BARE BACKBONES
A BRIEF INTRODUCTION TO ANTHROPOLOGY

FIRST EDITION

By Renée M. Bonzani
University of Kentucky

Bassim Hamadeh, CEO and Publisher
Michael Simpson, Vice President of Acquisitions
Jamie Giganti, Senior Managing Editor
Miguel Macias, Graphic Designer
Angela Schultz, Senior Field Acquisitions Editor
Michelle Piehl, Project Editor
Alexa Lucido, Licensing Coordinator
Allie Kiekhofer, Interior Designer

First published in the United States of America in 2016 by Cognella, Inc.

Printed in the United States of America

ISBN: 978-1-63189-670-5 (pbk) / 978-1-63189-671-2 (br)

www.cognella.com   800-200-3908

Contents

PART ONE
An Introduction to Anthropology

PART TWO
Physical or Biological Anthropology

PART THREE
Archaeology

PART FOUR
Linguistics

PART FIVE
Cultural Anthropology

Preface

Hopefully, this book can be utilized by students to help them understand some of the basic concepts found in textbooks providing an introduction to anthropology. These are brief notes that correspond to many of the chapters found in more thorough and extensive textbooks on the subject, and it is probably best if they are used in conjunction with more in-depth descriptions and case studies. A few chapters, such as those on territoriality, the industrial revolution, and politics and ideology, were added to try to better frame or explain the complex human relations covered in the chapters dealing with race and racism, ethnicity and nationalism, and globalization, to name a few.

After living on the Amazon River in Leticia, Colombia, and working for the Department of Children and Families in St. Petersburg, Florida, at the end of the 1990s, I moved to Lexington, Kentucky, and joined the Department of Anthropology at the University of Kentucky as a part-time Instructor, thanks to the help of Dr. Tom Dillehay (Vanderbilt University). Since then, I have been promoted to a Lecturer with the Department, and I have taught an Introduction to Anthropology and other undergraduate first-year anthropology courses for more than thirteen consecutive years. That is not much compared to some of the great professors and colleagues I have met, studied with, and worked with over the years. The list could go on and on.

I would like to thank Dr. Augusto Oyuela-Caycedo (University of Florida, Gainesville) and Dr. Erin Ricci (United States Agency for International Development) especially for their help with some of these notes when I first taught an Introduction to Anthropology and Cultural Anthropology. I would also like to thank the faculty and staff members at both the Department of Anthropology at the University of Kentucky and the Department of Anthropology, Sociology, and Social Work at Eastern Kentucky University for giving me the opportunity to improve my teaching and research skills and to compile all of this information for students over the years, and thanks to my many Teaching Assistants at the University of Kentucky who have helped me refine and teach much of this material. Also a great amount of appreciation is given to the acquisitions editor and editorial personnel who have greatly helped me with the publication of this book.

The information provided by these scholars has been added to and reconfigured over time as I have taught this course and found that students needed more or less information on a topic. The order of the chapters can also be easily rearranged for specific purposes, though I like the flow and construction of the chapters' order herein as we go through and build upon the various aspects of the four subfields of Anthropology. I also have not included many illustrations that I would have liked to, since the copyright permissions would have added greatly to the costs of publication, and instead, I have tried to find public domain photos and illustrations for use in this introductory text. I have also included some references for further reading, but this list is in no way exhaustive, as the bibliography itself would have then been most likely longer than the actual text! I assume that ten years from now, many, if not all, of the basic concepts defined in this book will remain the same yet the examples, research, reconfiguration, and methods for teaching this information will continue to advance through time. I look forward to seeing the new research and approaches in anthropology, and I hope, again, that students taking their first or second anthropology class, especially those in Introduction to Anthropology, will find this book very helpful.

Dedication

I would like to thank and dedicate this book to my family, including my parents, James S. and Rogene O. Bonzani; my sister and late brother, Lori and Jimmy; my children, Isabel and Marcel; my Uncles, John (Jack) and William (Bill) and Aunt Audrey; and Roger Owens for all of their love, help, and patience over these years.

List of Figures

List of Tables

PART ONE

Introduction to Anthropology

CHAPTER ONE

What is Anthropology?

- Anthropology: the scientific study of human beings, including their origins, distribution, physical attributes, and culture.
- Anthropology is comprised of four subfields: physical or biological anthropology, cultural anthropology, linguistics, and archaeology.
- Physical or Biological anthropology: the study of the origins and evolution of human beings and how and why modern human populations vary biologically.
- Cultural anthropology: the study of the culture or customary ways of thinking and behaving in different societies.
- Linguistics: the study of languages.
- Archaeology: the study of past human societies and cultures and their changes through time.

History of the Origins of Anthropology: Imperialism

Travelers, Missionary Accounts, Colonial Reports

- Empires always collect information on the people they subjugate for purposes of taxation and control.
- Only in the nineteenth century did the discipline of anthropology develop.
- The British and French empires initiated the collection of information on the "other" in a systematic way.

- Initially, anthropology was at the service of the empires.
- The advances in biology (taxonomy), geology (stratigraphy in archaeology), and economic studies created a basis for the development of anthropology as a discipline.

Factors That Influenced the Rise of Anthropology

- The desire to understand the variation in customs in the colonies demanded a clear knowledge of exotic customs, such as those involving marriage and religion.
- In the past, the curiosity of those who were colonized was aroused due to the development of urban areas and monumental architecture observed in these regions. Example: The ruins of the Egyptians, Persians, and Inca.
- The need to manage the colonized people demanded an understanding of the legal structures that these peoples had.
- That is why early works in anthropology were written by lawyers, such as Sir Henry Sumner Maine who published a comparative study entitled *Ancient Law* in 1861.
- Another lawyer was Lewis H. Morgan who is known as the father of U.S. anthropology.
- His most important works were on the study of kinship and on the evolution of society.

U.S. Cultural Anthropology Roots

Lewis H. Morgan

- Lewis H. Morgan (1818–1881). Born in Rochester, New York.
- Main books: *League of the Iroquois* (1851), *Systems of Consanguinity and Affinity of the Human Family* (1871), and *Ancient Society* (1877).
- Proposed the evolution of societies in three periods: Savagery, Barbarism, and Civilization.
- Unilineal evolutionist.
- Morgan had influence on Karl Marx, as is evident in his notebooks and texts.
- Morgan creates the basis of kinship studies.

- Today, instead of using the term civilization or the rise of civilizations, one more likely would hear of the development of complex societies.
- "Complex societies are those in which hierarchically ordered social components exhibit marked functional differentiation and specialization. The components are therefore functionally interdependent in that no individual or group can fulfill all of the required roles and duties." (Carmichael 1995, 181).

Timeline Illustrating Markers of Developing Complexity

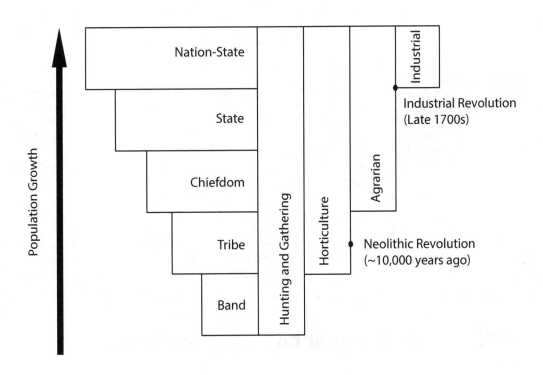

FIGURE 1.1. Timeline illustrating markers of developing complexity. Adapted from a class taught on industrial and non-industrial societies at the Department of Anthropology, Sociology, and Social Work, at Eastern Kentucky University in Richmond, Kentucky.

Table 1.1. Five Basic Components of Human Societies in Hunter-Gatherer, Horticultural/Pastoral, and Agricultural/Industrial Groups

Type of Society	Population	Culture	Material Products	Social/ Economic Organization	Social Institu- tions/ Institu- tional Systems
Hunter-Gatherers	Small, 50-100 individuals	Group identity markers	Rudimentary, stone/plant/ bone tools	Egalitarian, achieved status, generalized ("the gift") exchange	Kinship, band, extended family, animism, social mechanisms of behavior control
Horticultural/ Pastoral	Medium, 5,000-10,000 or more individuals	Group identity and territorial markers, ideologies of cults to the ancestors	Rudimentary, stone/plant/ bone tools	Ranked, start of ascribed status, generalized and balanced exchange	Kinship, Tribe, lineages and clans, animism and totemism, social/ideological mechanisms of behavioral control, arbitration
Agrarian	Large, over 10,000 to hundreds of thousands of individuals	Group identity and territorial markers, status differentiation, ideological group markers	Plow, milling devices, metallurgy	Stratified, ascribed/ achieved status, classes/ castes, general-ized, balanced and negative exchanges	Chiefdoms and states, theocra-cies/nobility (ruler believed to be a God), rule-centered legal codes
Industrial	Large, hundreds of thousands of individuals	Nationalism ethnic groups	Industrial machines, non-renew-able energy sources	Negative exchanges, market-place based	Shift toward democracies and individual human rights, rule-centered legal codes

The Rise of the Cultural Anthropology School

Franz Boas

- Franz Boas (1858–1942). Founder of the first university department of anthropology in the U.S. at Clark University in 1888. He was a Professor at Columbia and conducted a study of the Kwakiutl and the potlatch.
- Born in Germany; was a geographer and curator of the field museum at Chicago and later New York.

The German Influence on Boas

- Friedrich Ratzel (1804–1944), the Kulturkrise school, anthropogeography book. Publications: *The History of Mankind* (1896); also see *Völkerkunde,* volume 3 (1885–1888).
- Diffusionism
- Environmental determinism
- Theodor Waitz (1821–1864), the unity of the human mind in *Anthropologie der naturvölker* (1859).
- Adolphe Bastian (1826–1905). German. Teacher of Franz Boas.

Boas' Contribution to Anthropology

- Boas attacked the idea of cross-cultural comparison, as well as unilineal evolution and the eugenics movement. He condemned cross-cultural comparison and unilineal evolution in 1916, indicating that the psychological basis of cultural traits is identical in all races and that the same cultural traits in different societies could arise from numerous pathways.
- Boas promoted the conception of cultural relativism: all cultures are equal and comparable; there are no inferior or superior cultures.
- Asserted that it is impossible to order cultures in an evolutionary scheme.
- Publications: *The Mind of Primitive Man* (1911) and several others.
- Promoted fieldwork with groups under study, as with the Jesup Expedition (1897).

Other Influences in U.S. Anthropology

Karl Marx

- Karl Marx (1818–1883). Publication: *Capital* (1867).
- Outlined the unilineal evolution of society from primitive communism to capitalism and socialism in progressive stages.

Herbert Spencer

- Herbert Spencer (1812–1903). Studied the evolution of society, unilineal evolution, and principles of sociology.
- Promoted the concept of "survival of the fittest," whereby society is seen as a system that has structure and functions. The evolution of society is based on its structural differentiation. Society is seen as an organism.

Edward Burnett Tylor

- Edward Burnett Tylor (1832–1917). Publication: *Primitive Culture* (1871).
- Studied and wrote on the origins of religion, sacrifice, and animism.
- Savagery - Promiscuous - Animism.
- Barbarism - Polygamy - Polytheism.
- Civilization - Monogamy - Monotheism.

- James G. Frazer (1854–1941). Publications: *The Golden Bough* (1890), which is a study in magic and religion (12 volumes), and *Totemism and Exogamy* (1910).

Influences of Sociology and Other Scholars

Emile Durkheim

- Emile Durkheim (1858–1907). Publication: *The Division of Labor in Society* (1893).
- Uses an analogy where a society functions like an organism that seeks to fulfill its needs for survival, for instance.
- Defines the difference between mechanical solidarity and organic solidarity.

- Mechanical solidarity (archaic form of solidarity): societies organized in clans are examples of mechanical solidarity.
- Organic solidarity: a product of the development of the division of labor.
- Collective or common conscience: the totality of beliefs and sentiments common to the average citizen, which forms a determinate system having a life of its own.

- The internal differentiation of the society favors the rise of individuality and complexity in what is called *organic solidarity*. Each organ has to work together to maintain the organism, for example, in state societies.

Max Weber: Father of Sociology

- Max Weber (1864–1920). Publications: *The Sociology of Religion* (1922), *The Protestant Ethic and the Spirit of Capitalism* (1930 [1904–1905, 1920]), and *Agrarian Sociology of Ancient Civilization* (1976 [1897, 1889, 1909]).
- Conceptual contribution include: ideal types, social action and charismatic power, superstructure, and the role of ideology.

Arnold van Gennep

- Arnold van Gennep (1873–1957). Born in Germany.
- Publication: *The Rites of Passage* (1908).
- Worked on totemism, comparison of rites and myths.
- Conducted a study of the folklore of rural France.

Marcel Mauss

- Marcel Mauss (1872–1950). French sociologist/anthropologist.
- Publication: *The Gift: Forms and Functions of Exchange in Archaic Societies* (1966).
- Dealing with gift exchange and: 1) the obligation to give, 2) the obligation to receive, and 3) the obligation to repay.

- Many of these ideas will be reintroduced in latter parts of the guide.

CHAPTER TWO

Methods and Theory in Anthropology

Introduction

- Two basic ways to study different peoples and societies include doing an ethnography or ethnology.
- Ethnography is the systematic and scientific study of the way of life of one particular society, including subsistence, kinship patterns, economics, politics, and religion.
- Ethnology is the comparative study of two or more societies.

- Researchers doing either may use the Human Relations Area Files to obtain information on numerous topics concerning indigenous and ethnic groups today and in the past (http://hraf.yale.edu/).

- Basic ethnographic field techniques include:
  1. Participant observation
  2. Interviews
  3. Genealogical methods and recording
  4. Close interactions and work with key consultants or informants
  5. Collection of life histories
  6. Hypothesis testing and research
  7. Long term study of an area or site
  8. Team and interdisciplinary research of an area or site

- All Anthropologists should adhere, to the best of their abilities, to the American Anthropological Association (AAA) Code of Ethics, as found in the AAA website (www.aaanet.org/cmtes/ethics/Ethics-Resources.cfm) and described in Kottak (2013:85-87).

Statement on Ethics

- Principles of Professional Responsibility as developed by the American Anthropological Association:
  1. Do No Harm
  2. Be Open and Honest Regarding Your Work
  3. Obtain Informed Consent and Necessary Permissions
  4. Weigh Competing Ethical Obligations Due Collaborators and Affected Parties
  5. Make Your Results Accessible
  6. Protect and Preserve Your Records
  7. Maintain Respectful and Ethical Professional Relationships

Major Theoretical Orientations in Anthropology

- Specific information found in Kottak (2013, 285–295).
  1. Unilinear evolutionism is the concept that all societies follow a single line or course of cultural development. Developed by Lewis Henry Morgan (1877) and Edward Tylor (1871).
  2. Historical particularism is the concept that the histories of different societies are not comparable but that these diverse paths can lead to the same cultural manifestation. Developed by Franz Boas (1940) and his students.
  3. Functionalism is the concept that socio-cultural practices have a function in the social systems in which they are found. Developed by Bronislaw Malinowski (1944, 1922).
  4. Structural functionalism is the concept that sociocultural practices function to preserve the structure of the system, made up of different parts, as a whole. Developed by A. R. Radcliffe-Brown (1952) and E.E. Evans-Pritchard (1940).
  5. Configurationalism is the concept that culture is integrated and patterned. Developed by Ruth Benedict (1934), Alfred Kroeber (1944), and Margaret Mead (1935).
  6. Culturology is the scientific study of cultural anthropology. Developed by Leslie White (1949).
  7. Practice or action theory is the approach to culture that recognizes that individuals within a society vary in their beliefs, intentions, and motives and in the amount of power and influence that they have. Developed by The

Manchester School and Edmund Leach (1954), Victor Turner (1957), Sherry Ortner (1984), and Pierre Bourdieu (1977).

8. Neoevolutionism is the concept that societies or different cultures evolve through time, albeit not necessarily along the same trajectories, and it is associated with cultural ecology, which considers the relationships between cultures and environmental variables. Developed by Leslie White (1959) and Julian Steward (1955).

9. Structuralism is the concept that all human minds have certain universal characteristics and that these lead people everywhere to think similarly and to develop certain similar cultural structures or manifestations, such as in kinship and marriage systems. Developed by Claude Lévi-Strauss (1967).

10. Symbolic anthropology is the study of symbols in their social and cultural contexts. Developed by Mary Douglas (1970) and Victor Turner (1967).

11. Interpretive anthropology is the study of a culture as a system of meaning. Developed by Clifford Geertz (1973).

12. Cultural materialism is the concept that a cultural infrastructure is what determines the structure and superstructure of a culture and that this infrastructure is a cultural core consisting of technology, economics, and demography upon which the rest of the cultural structure—social relations, forms of kinship, and patterns of distribution and consumption— and superstructure—religion, ideology, and play—are developed. (Marvin Harris 1979, 1968).

13. Feminist anthropology is an approach that focuses on cultural issues related to females and gender relations. Developed by Rayna Reiter (1975) and Michelle Rosaldo and Louise Lamphere (1974).

14. World-system theory or political economy is a concept that includes the inter-relations of economics and power in a society and is framed in the context of a world system where socio-political and economic relations can be viewed in terms of core, periphery, and semi-periphery interactions. Developed by Sidney Mintz (1985) and Eric Wolf (1982), also see Immanuel Wallerstein (2004).

15. Postmodernism is an approach that covers power relations but focuses more on local agency—the actions of individuals together or alone that create and transform cultures—with the individuals and groups often within colonized societies. Developed by Jean François Lyotard (1993) and George Marcus and Michael Fischer (1986).

16. Culture, history, and power are identified as a theoretical approach that focuses on systems of power, domination, accommodation, and resistance in various contexts. Developed by Ann Stoler (2002) and Frederick Cooper and Ann Stoler (1997).

PART TWO

Physical or Biological Anthropology

CHAPTER THREE

From Genetic Diversity to Human Variation

- Why, as humans, are we so diverse?
- Biological or genetic diversity
- Mechanisms

The Basic Strands or Codes of Life

- The human body is made up of cells. Each cell has a nucleus. Within the nucleus are strands of DNA.
- DNA: deoxyribonucleic acid. A double helix formation that contains the codes for the formation and functions of a living organism. It is composed of building blocks called nucleotides.
- Nucleotides: the building blocks of DNA. There are four kinds of building blocks. Two of the bases are adenine and guanine, and the other two are cytosine and thymine. These are arranged in a sequence with cytosine bonding only to guanine and thymine bonding only to adenine.

- Chromosomes: strands of DNA found in the nucleus. This structure is where the genetic information, or genes, are located. A human cell contains twenty-three pairs of chromosomes (or forty-six chromosomes). Pairs of chromosomes that line up together are called homologous chromosomes.
- Gene: basic unit of genetic information or inheritance. A portion of a DNA molecule that codes for a product, like a protein.
- Alleles: the different forms of a gene, when a gene exists in more than one form. Represented as a letter. A capital letter indicates dominance, and a small letter indicates recessive traits. For homologous chromosomes, the same alleles on each chromosome or different alleles on each chromosome may occur.
- Homozygous: cells with the same alleles, either dominant, TT, or recessive, tt.
- Heterozygous: cells with different alleles, Tt.
- Genotype: the genetic composition, TT, tt, Tt.
- Phenotype: the appearance represented by the genetic composition, TT and Tt (same appearance).

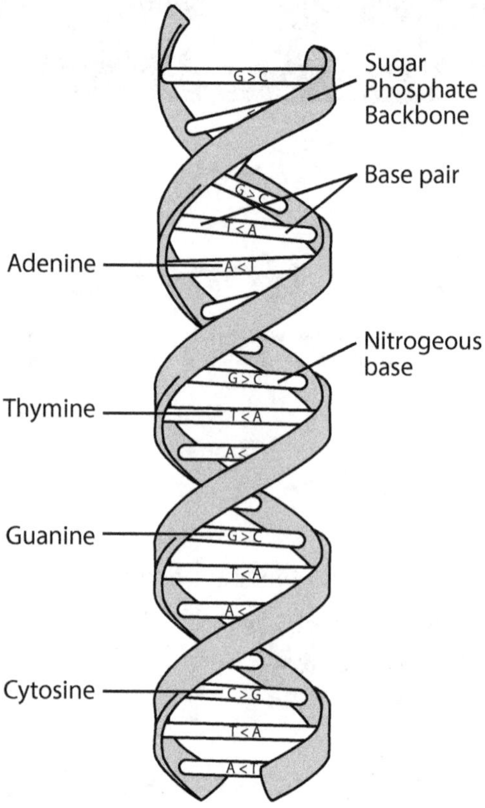

FIGURE 3.1. The separation and replication of DNA.
Copyright © William T. Keeton (CC BY-SA 3.0) at https://dnabiob.wikispaces.com/Watson+%26+Crick.

Combination and Recombination

- How is genetic information passed on in cells and from parents to offspring (Keeton 1976)?
- Mitosis: the division of cells. Nuclear division is, first, the complete replication of all of the chromosomes in a cell and, second, the distribution of a complete set of chromosomes to each daughter cell. Thus each daughter cell has twenty-three

pairs of chromosomes (or forty-six chromosomes) in humans, or it is said to be diploid.

- Diploid: having two sets of the same chromosomes.
- Meiosis: the sexual division of cells. Each cell only contains half of the typical number of chromosomes. Chromosomes are not duplicated, but homologous pairs are separated into different gamete cells. This separation occurs twice and results in four haploid cells. Each gamete cell has twenty-three chromosomes in humans.
- Haploid: having one set of chromosomes.
- Gamete cells: sperm and egg cells. Sexual reproduction results in the recombination of the twenty-three chromosomes in the egg cell with the twenty-three homologous chromosomes in the sperm cell, resulting in forty-six chromosomes or twenty-three chromosome pairs in humans. The offspring has one set of the twenty-three chromosomes from the mother and one set of the chromosomes from the father.
- Cloning: the replication of the chromosomes without the recombination of haploid gamete cells. This is known to occur in asexual reproduction through mitosis. The result is that the offspring has the exact same genetic makeup as the parent.

CHAPTER FOUR

Population Diversity, Migration, and Environmental Diversity From Genetic Diversity to Human Variation

- Evolution can be seen as changes in the genetic makeup of populations over time.

How Do Genetic Changes Get Passed from One Individual (Parent) to Another (Offspring)?

Mendelian Genetics

- Mendelian genetics: Gregor Mendel was an Austrian monk who, from 1856 to 1868, preformed experiments with ordinary garden peas. The results were published in *Versuche Über Pflanzenhybriden* in 1866.
- He found that, if he crossed a red flowered pea with a white flowered pea, the first generation was all red (F1 generation; 100% red). However, the second generation (F2 generation) had three red offspring and one white offspring (75% red, 25% white).

- If we review our concepts from the last chapter:
- Gene: basic unit of genetic information or inheritance. A portion of a DNA molecule that codes for some product, like a protein.
- Alleles: the different forms of a gene, when a gene exists in more than one form. Represented as a letter. A capital letter indicates dominance, and a small letter indicates recessive traits. For homologous chromosomes, the same allele on each chromosome or different alleles on each chromosome may occur.

- Homozygous: cells with the same alleles, either dominant, CC, or recessive, cc.
- Heterozygous: cells with different alleles, Cc.
- Heterozygous: cells with different alleles, cC.

- From Mendel's experiments then:
- Using capital C: dominant allele, red color.
- Using lowercase c: recessive allele, white color.
- Red flower is CC, white flower is cc. Homozygous.
- Red flower is Cc or cC. Heterozygous.

	C	C (red)	P Generation
c	Cc	Cc	F1 individuals all heterozygous plants, red flowered
c	Cc	Cc	

(white)

	C	c (red)	
C	CC	cC	F2 individuals two homozygous and two heterozygous plants, 75 % red flowered and 25 % white flowered
c	Cc	cc	

(red)

- Genotype: the genetic composition, CC, cc, Cc.
- Phenotype: the appearance represented by the genetic composition, CC and Cc (same appearance).
- This is how genes are passed on and is the basis for genetic diversity in organisms.

How and Why are Genetic Changes Expressed in a Population

- Three factors to be covered herein that make individuals and populations different biologically:

- Mutation: random change to the DNA structure or genetic code.
- Natural Selection: survival of the fittest. Acts on traits that benefit the adaptation of the species to their environment.

- Genetic drift: changes in the gene pool purely as a result of chance and not as a result of selection, mutation, or migration.
- A fourth factor, not addressed in this chapter, is that of sexual selection whereby selection favors characteristics that increase mating success. This fourth factor will be addressed in the next chapter with an example dealing with humans.

Natural Selection

- The theory of evolution by natural selection was formulated by Charles Darwin and A. R. Wallace. Charles Darwin published *The Origins of Species* in 1859.
- See information on Charles Darwin in Strickberger (1990).
- Darwin and Wallace recognized the heritable variation as *characters* passed on by the parents. However, they did not know of Mendel's work, in which it was recognized that the unit of selection was the gene that behaves in a predictable manner.
- They observed the persistence of characters that benefited the adaptation of the species to their environments.
- Wallace and Darwin recognized the gradualism of environmental changes.
- Evolution by means of natural selection was, for Darwin and Wallace, just the differential reproductive success of the species and the adaptation to changing environments where adaptive characters are perpetuated and non-adaptive ones are eliminated.
- Darwin and Wallace did not know how the characters were produced. Only when genetics was developed was it possible to understand this.

Darwin and Wallace's Evolutionary Process

- Every species on this planet arose through the same process.
- This process defines why a species looks and behaves a certain way. This process affects morphology, physiology, and behavior.
- Humans are subject to the same evolutionary process.

Postulates

1. The ability of a population to expand is infinite, while the resources available to sustain the population are finite. This dynamic causes a struggle for existence among individuals as they compete for resources.
2. Organisms vary in their physical qualities; these variations allow some members to survive and reproduce more successfully than others (producing more offspring) in the same environment.
3. These variations are inherited by offspring from their parents. Thus, traits that confer an advantage in survival and reproduction are retained in the population, and traits that are disadvantageous disappear.

- Natural selection preserves the status quo when the most common type is the best adapted.
- Natural selection operates even over short time periods. Example: Changes from the probable ancestor of maize, teosinte (*Zea mays* ssp. *parviglumis*) to maize (*Zea mays* ssp. *mays*) may have only occurred over a few generations.
- Archaeological evidence of corn's evolution:
- Genotypic and phenotypic changes from the earliest recovered small corn cobs (about 2 centimeters [cm]) to corn cobs over 12 cm in length may have taken less than 6,000 years. Example: Bat Cave, New Mexico (earliest cobs date ca. 2300 BC) (Dick 1965; Manglesdorf 1974; Manglesdorf et al. 1967).
- Figure from Manglesdorf (1974: Figure 14.1, 150) illustrates: (A) Three cobs or possible fragments of cobs found in the lowest levels of the excavations at Bat Cave, dated to ca. 2300 BC (B) A series of Chapalote-type cobs, the shortest being from the lower levels of Bat Cave at 48 cm to 60 cm with the longest cobs from the 12 inches (in) to 24 in.

Where Does Selection Operate?

- Adaptation operates at the level of individuals who compete for resources and reproductive success. This is also important when we look at individual decision-making in terms of cultural adaptation.
- Selection produces adaptations that favor individuals, not populations or species.
- Adaptation favors the fitness of the individual.

What is Fitness?

- Fitness is reproductive success of an individual. In other words, it is the number of offspring that an individual has.
- Fitness is different and should not be confused with fecundity, which is the ability to produce offspring.
- It is the accumulation and random selection of traits that produce adaptive changes and the evolution of species. This is called *continuous variation.*
- Adaptation and fitness operate at the level of individuals.

Summary

- Natural selection, acting over time, can work only if each small change along the way is, itself, adaptive.
- Evolution of species is a product of adaptation to changing conditions by a process of natural selection.
- Natural selection can be summarized as the process of differential reproductive success of individuals.
- Darwin's explanation of variation can easily incorporate the genetic view that evolution typically results from changes in gene frequencies.
- Gene frequencies: the percentage of a population that has a particular allelic composition of a gene for a trait. Gene frequencies show continuous variation within a population.
- Natural Selection acts on genetic variation in an environment only when it is expressed as phenotypic variation. In different environments, different genetic makeups are more adaptive to the population (those individuals with the greatest fitness) and will get passed on to offspring.

CHAPTER FIVE

The Importance of Migration and Adaptation in Genetic Diversity

How and Why are Genetic Changes Expressed in a Population

- Let's review from the last chapter:
- Three factors discussed herein that make individuals and populations different biologically:
- Mutation: random change to the DNA structure or genetic code.
- Natural Selection: the survival of the fittest. Acts on traits that benefit the adaptation of the species to their environment.
- Genetic drift: changes in the gene pool purely as a result of chance, and not as a result of selection, mutation, or migration.
- A fourth factor, that of sexual selection, whereby selection favors characteristics that increase mating success, will be addressed with an example later in this chapter.

Mutations and the Environment: Why are They Sometimes Maintained in Low Frequency and Not Eliminated by Natural Selection?

- The maintenance of different genotypes through heterozygote superiority of selection is called balanced polymorphism.
- An example of this comes from Cavalli-Sforza and Cavalli-Sforza (1996).

- Mutations: random change to the DNA structure or genetic code. One mechanism for genetic diversity to occur. Mutations are usually deleterious and do not get passed on to the next generation, because offspring die before reaching the age of reproduction. However some diseases caused by genetic mutations do not occur until after the reproductive age and can get passed to offspring.

Thalassemia

- Question: why do recessive deleterious alleles that often result in lethal diseases remain in a population?
- Example: thalassemia or Mediterranean anemia affecting the red blood cells.
- N: normal; T: mutation that causes the anemia:

	N	T
N	NN	NT
T	NT	TT

- 75% normal (one homozygous, two heterozygous)
- 25% diseased (one homozygous)
- The heterozygous individuals have an advantage when affected by malaria.
- Natural selection favors the NT individuals in areas with malaria. Thus they continue to produce in the population at large.
- What is another example related to this?

Sickle Cell Anemia

- Just as directional selection can reduce variety, it can also maintain genetic variety by favoring a situation in which the frequency of certain alleles remain constant between generations.

- Hemoglobin in Africa
- Hb^A and Hb^S are two alleles for a gene that largely determine hemoglobin production in humans.
- Homozygous Hb^A produces normal hemoglobin.
- Homozygous Hb^S produces lethal sickle cell anemia.

- Heterozygosity for this gene (in some circumstances) produces the deleterious but nonlethal sickle-cell syndrome.
- It was discovered, in certain populations in Africa, India, and the Mediterranean, that that Hb^S allele existed at surprisingly high frequencies.
- This is largely explained by the fact that the populations noted were in areas greatly affected by malaria and that the heterozygous form produced a phenotype that was resistant to malaria and was, thus, the phenotype most fit for that environment.

Hb^A/Hb^A homozygote, normal red blood cells

Hb^A/Hb^S heterozygote, deleterious non-lethal sickle cell syndrome

Hb^S/Hb^S homozygote, lethal sickle cell anemia

 Person has one child, gets malaria, and dies.

 Person has one child, gets malaria, recovers, and has three more children.

 Person dies before having children.

- The presence of two alleles that are heterozygotes Hb^A/Hb^S allows an individual to survive the malaria parasite more successfully than do either normal Hb^A/Hb^A or sickle-cell homozygotes Hb^s/Hb^s.
- This is an example of how the environment that these populations live in will affect their phenotype and genotype.
- Further examples of how the environment affects genotypes and phenotypes of populations will follow.

Effects of Migration and Adaptation on Genetic Diversity

Genetic Drift

Genetic Drift

- Genetic drift: changes in the gene pool purely as a result of chance, and not as a result of selection, mutation, or migration.
- Example: the genetic composition of the island of Pitcairn in the Pacific, which was founded by six British sailors and a similar number of Melanesian or Polynesian women. The offspring of all following generations were limited to the genetic composition of these founders.

Founders' Effect

- Founders' effect: when only a few founders populate an area, and their genetic composition is different from that of earlier peoples. A rare genetic disease in the general population may be quite common in these isolated groups.
- Another example: most Native Americans have O as their blood group. One possible explanation for this is that, by a process of chance or genetic drift, the first settlers of the Americas all had this same blood group (O). Only later, after the time of Columbus, did peoples with different blood groups (A, B, AB) migrate into the New World.

- From the Stanford University School of Medicine Blood Center Press Kit http://bloodcenter.stanford.edu/press/press_kit.html
- What is the most common blood type?
- The approximate distribution of blood types in the U.S. population is as follows. Distribution may be different for specific racial and ethnic groups:

New World blood types prior to A.D. 1492	Type O	ca. 100%		
US blood types present day	O Rh-positive	38%	B Rh-positive	9%
	O Rh-negative	7%	B Rh-negative	2%
	A Rh-positive	34%	AB Rh-positive	3%
	A Rh-negative	6%	AB Rh-negative	1%

Table 5.1. Blood Types
"Blood Types," http://bloodcenter.stanford.edu/press/press_kit.html. Copyright in the Public Domain.

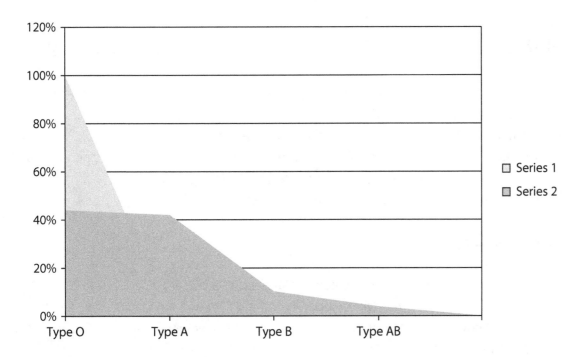

FIGURE 5.1. Graph illustrating the influence of gene flow and migration on blood types. Light grey (Series 1) indicates approximate percentage of persons with blood types in the New World prior to AD 1492; dark grey (Series 2) indicates percentage of persons with different blood types currently in the United States.

- With migration into an area, new genetic material is introduced, and one sees more continuous variation in traits and a modulation around the most adaptive traits.

Gene flow

- Gene flow occurs through interbreeding—the transmission of genetic material from one population to another.
- Gene flow inhibits speciation—the formation of new species.
- Speciation can be defined as the inability of different populations to interbreed.

- Gene frequencies: the percentage of a population that has a particular allelic composition of a gene for a trait. Gene frequencies show continuous variation within a population.
- Natural Selection acts on genetic variation in an environment only when it is expressed as phenotypic variation. In different environments, different genetic makeups are more adaptive to the population (those individuals with the greatest fitness) and will get passed on to offspring.

Natural Selection: Human Variation and Environment

- All humans have the same basic genetic code (i.e., forty-six chromosomes or twenty-three pairs of chromosomes).
- The frequencies of the alleles they have for genes are different.
- Natural selection works on the phenotype, and therefore, differences in phenotypes are what we can see and what are expressed by the genotypes.
- More examples of human variation and the environment:

Example: Body Size

- Body size and temperature. In colder climates, it is better to be large to limit the amount of heat lost through the body. In warmer climates it is better to be smaller. When body volume increases, the ratio of surface to volume diminishes, and heat generated by the body is lost more slowly.
- Bergmann's rule: Larger bodies occur in colder climates, while smaller ones are found in warmer climates.
- Allen's rule: Longer protruding body parts are expected to occur in warmer climates.

Example: Body Fat and Temperature

- Humans are genetically well adapted to hot, dry conditions. There is no evidence of different genetic adaptations to heat in different populations. In relation to cold, humans have very low tolerance for cold. The protection to cold depends on the thickness of the layer of fat under the skin.

Example: Lactose Intolerance

- The term phenotypic adaptation refers to changes occurring to an individual organism during its lifetime that enhance its reproductive fitness.
- Individuals from herding populations in Northern Europe and parts of Africa maintain their ability to digest milk (continue to produce the enzyme lactase) into adulthood, whereas people from other populations can digest milk (specifically, milk sugar, called lactose) only during childhood.
- The fact that descendants of these herding populations who no longer herd continue to be lactose tolerant as adults indicates genetic adaptation to a milk-rich diet.

FIGURE 5.2. Witoto sellers at marketplace, Leticia, Department of Amazonas, Colombia, (ca. 1998) (Photo by Renée M. Bonzani).

Example: Pigments of the Skin

- Melanocytes produce melanin pigment. The more pigment in the skin, the darker the skin.
- Explanations of how sunlight affects the body in terms of the amount of skin pigmentation:

1. Protection from skin cancer.
2. Dark skin protects the body's folate stores (folic acid) from destruction.
3. Ultraviolet (UV) light initiates the formation of vitamin D. Deficiency in this vitamin can result in poor ossification of bone and skeletal deformation or rickets.

- Dark pigmentation keeps out harmful ultraviolet rays from the sun. In areas around the Equator, where there is more direct sunlight, it is an adaptive advantage to have dark skin. Natural selection in this environment means that individuals with darker skin will have higher fitness (less likely to get skin cancer, for instance) or will produce more offspring.

- Light pigmentation allows UV radiation to be absorbed by the skin. Absorption of UV rays allows for precursors of vitamin D to be broken down in the body, aiding the absorption of calcium and the development of bones. Light skin is favored in areas where there is less sunlight and where natural forms of vitamin D (meat, fish liver) are limited. Natural selection in this environment means that individuals with light skin will have higher fitness or will produce more offspring.

FIGURE 5.3. Norwegians harvesting oats, Jølston ca. 1890. Photo taken by Axel Theodor Lindahl (1841–1906)/Norwegian Museum of Cultural History *Axel Lindahl, "Harvesting Oats, Norway," http://www.nb.no/cgi-bin/galnor/gn_sok.sh?id=51139&skjema=2&fm=4. Copyright in the Public Domain.*

What about Sexual Selection?

Genetic Research and Basic Premise

- In his article, Frost (2014) asks if there is just a simple correlation between skin color and amount of UV radiation, then what about populations living in the far northern and southern latitudes that have brown skin?
- And, why do only European populations have such variability when it comes to hair and eye color?

- Genetic research shows three genes and "new" alleles affect light skin color.
- Eleven alleles at a genetic region affect hair color for people from Europe, five alleles for people from Asia, and one allele for people from Africa.
- Other new alleles in one genetic region affect eye color though the exact number of alleles that do this still needs to be determined.
- Research is indicating that eye color diversification occurred before hair color diversification and the lightening of skin color in this area of the world (i.e., Europe).

- The answers to the questions above rest on the basic premise that both males and females compete for mates.
- All else being equal (such as the ability to have offspring), how does one sex attract a mate in a competitive environment?
- The answer may be visual stimuli, especially for females, involving the face, with sexual dimorphism also becoming more pronounced (such as wider hips, narrower waists, and thicker subcutaneous fat).

The Setting

- The environments of Europe and central Asia from 40,000 to 10,000 years ago, when humans (*Homo sapiens sapiens*) are identified as first occurring in these areas, were steppe-tundra, or cold with very little plant biomass.
- In these types of environments, it is hard to acquire food.
- Women cannot easily go out to forage for plants on a daily basis or have small gardens year round.

- For men, it takes a lot of effort to get food by hunting and fishing, just to take care of one woman and offspring.

- Therefore unlike in tropical regions where women supply a lot of the food and men can be polygamous (take care of two or more wives and offspring) in steppe-tundra environments, these aspects of culture are unlikely or are much more difficult.

- These environments are also assumed to lead to a high risk of early male death as a result of hunting reindeer and other animals far from home and for extended periods of time.

- This is assumed to have led to an imbalance in the numbers of men and women for mating, with women outnumbering men.

What Might Have Been an Outcome of These Factors?

- New mutations in hair and eye color would be more exotic and eye catching, and a person with these characteristics would be chosen for mating over others.

- With mating and reproduction, these novel characteristics would be passed on to the next generations until they were as "normal" as brown skin, brown eyes, and brown hair, and another mutation would occur. (Side question: what would have caused these mutations in the first place?)

- This is assumed to have occurred more in women, since they would "need" (or sexual selection would favor) some mechanism to attract one of the lesser numbers of males.

- Hence, in these European and Central Asian contexts, new color combinations are expected (and apparently) did occur as a form of "enticing" sexual selection.

- For skin color, studies indicate that females in general and in all populations tend to have lighter skin color, including hue and luminosity, than males, and this seems to be a characteristic that has been sexually selected for over time in many populations.

- In Europe and Central Asia, this appears to have occurred to the point that some Europeans are considered to be "milky-white" and are as close to the threshold of skin depigmentation as possible in relation to UV radiation protection.

- Perhaps, here, we see the combination of natural selection and sexual selection occurring together in dark, colder environments to lead to the phenotypic characteristics (skin, hair, and eye color) seen in one population of the world.
- What do you think about this?

- Review the article by Frost (2014) to get more information on this issue.

Conclusions on Environment and Adaptation

- One single origin for the species *Homo sapiens* occurred. Discussion to follow.
- All humans are the same species.
- There are no races, just genetic variation that is related to adaptation to the environment.
- There is no biological basis to create groups of population in terms of distinctive genetic characteristics. We can observe variations in gene frequencies, but there are no exclusive genes relating a group by religion, geography, country/nationality, color, or any category.

CHAPTER SIX

The Individual, Social Identification, and Territoriality

Natural Selection

- As we know from previous chapters:
- Natural Selection: the survival of the fittest. Acts on traits that benefit the adaptation of the species to its environment.
- Adaptation operates at the *level of individuals* who compete for resources and reproductive success. This is also important when we look at individual decision making in terms of cultural adaptation.
- Fitness is the reproductive success of an individual. In other words, it is the number of offspring that an individual has, and it should be added, the offspring's ability to go on to reach their own reproductive years.

The Individual

- The individual is the unit upon which natural selection operates.
- Therefore, it is the decisions made by the individual that affect his/her fitness and reproductive success.
- These decisions help to determine the success of passing on the genetic code of a person.
- Since humans live in a social environment, the societal norms or rules (culture) in which a person lives will also be passed on by example and education to that person's offspring.

- Whichever parent is the primary caretaker of the offspring, that parent will be the primary example of the societal norms in which a child is born.
- Since it is generally the female who cares for the young, the societal norms in which she lives will be passed on or exemplified by her offspring with input from the male.
- Taken with qualifications, females are generally the most isolated or traditional members of the society.

Link to Our Ancestors and Primate Behavior

- Care of young extends over a long period, at least in evidence from remains of *Homo erectus*.
- Ratio of the size of mother's birth canal to baby's head is the same as in modern humans, leading to the conclusion that children were born before full brain development and needed extended parental care.

Territoriality

- Territory can be simply defined as "domain" or the extent of land under the control of a particular group.
- Territoriality is the collection of behaviors that occur in relation to the territory occupied by an individual and the groups to which he/she belongs.
- Territoriality has both a spatial and temporal component.
- The spatial component involves the base, ranges, and boundaries.
- The base (home of the individual, central location of the group) is the area that is most frequently occupied by the individual or group.
- The range is the area in which the individual or group travels.
- The boundaries are the borders of the range or territory through which the individual or group will infrequently pass.

- Spatial boundaries are affected by the types of societies in which one is born.
- All social institutions create forms of identity that also relate to the complexity of subsistence diversity. These can be identified at three levels of complexity:
    1. At the family level.

2. At the community level.
3. At the inter-community level. These societies are called bands, tribes, chief-doms, or states.

- Each has its own political, economic, and kinship structure and differences in the ways it moves within a territory.

Table 6.1. Expected Settlement Pattern and Range/Boundary Characteristics for Entities of Varying Sociopolitical Complexity

Sociopolitical complexity	Settlement Pattern	Range/Boundary Characteristics
Egalitarian	Dispersed	Fluid
Chiefdom (pre-state stratified)	Nucleated	Discrete (buffer zones present)
State (within borders)	Dispersed but compartmentalized	Discrete (single large center)

- The temporal component of territoriality is affected by external and internal forces to the individual and group to which he/she belongs.
- These include the environment, as, for instance, in yearly fluctuations, especially in terms of seasonality, and long-term fluctuations in terms of climatic change.
- The location of groups can vary based on seasonal availability of food.
- Various festivities vary over the course of the seasons of a year. These festivities often involve movements or pilgrimages of peoples and they can often be tied to major religious dates, such as Easter that always occurs at the beginning of the spring season in the Northern hemisphere or *Inti Raymi*, a religious Incan sun god festival that still occurs in some locations in the Andes Mountains in the Southern hemisphere during the winter solstice in June.
- Long term climatic change can also affect individual beliefs and group composition, as, for instance, in religious affiliation.
- Group pressure to make decisions that will affect future generations also plays a part in temporal territoriality.
- This pressure on decision making is especially noticeable when one looks at kinship affiliations and marriage practices.
- The kin groups that you belong to; the location where you live as a child and, later, as a married adult; and the individuals and groups you can marry into may all be regulated by your position at birth.
- This regulation of the space and temporal affiliations of an individual usually occur to maintain the control of the group over key resources (i.e., labor, land, and important areas where key resources, in terms of survival and/or economic gain, are located).

Changing Boundaries and Identities

- Of major importance: spatial boundaries of individuals in terms of both physical space and group affiliation fluctuate over time.
- Spatial boundaries of kinship groups, larger ethnic groups, and even states can fluctuate over time depending on external and internal influences.
- For instance, the individual may accept belonging to a group at a certain time, which allows access to certain areas. This individual may, later, change his or her mind and drop such an affiliation, changing the people and areas with which they associate.
- This also occurs at a group level; for instance, in indigenous groups who, based on external pressures to acquire their land, may begin to emphasize group affiliation through symbolic means and the territory in which they reside by demarcating boundaries.

Symbols and Symbolism

- Who are you? Who am I?
- Symbols are utilized to mark individual and group identities.
- Symbol: an object used to represent something abstract.
- Through the use of an object that conveys a certain meaning, individuals or groups can mark their identities as members of that group and not members of another group.
- Identity: who or what a person is.
- This differentiation between us and them seems to be a fundamental tenet in the relations between humans and between groups.

CHAPTER SEVEN

Conflicts that Occur Between Indigenous/Ethnic Identities and the State

Imagined Ex-Communities: Race and Its Social Constructions

- Definitions found in: Kottak and Kozaitis (2003).
- Race: a culturally defined category and manner of organizing human individuals and populations based on assumed shared physical (usually phenotypic) characteristics.
- Social race: groups assumed to have a biological basis, but actually, are defined in a culturally arbitrary, rather than scientific, manner.
- The concept of race is based on historic goals to classify all animals into groups (phylogeny).
- Later used as a tripartite system during the Colonial period (late 1800s to 1900s) to keep "white" Europeans separated from their "black" African and "yellow" Asian subjects.
- Such classifications attempt to place specific groups of people into isolated distinct groups and are supposed to reflect shared genetic (genotypic) material.
- However, such attempts have tended to use phenotypic traits (usually skin color) for racial classification, and these are the same traits used to assign arbitrary cultural values to groups.

- Race: the unsustainable invention of biological racial differences or the invention of unverifiable biological differences to categorize people into separate groups for varying reasons.
- Racism: beliefs about categorical superiority and inferiority of socially defined groups assumed to share biological characteristics.

- Intrinsic racism: the belief that a perceived racial (supposed biological) difference is a sufficient reason to value one person less than another.
- Stereotypes: fixed ideas, often unfavorable, about what members of a group are like.
- Racial classification from the biological perspective: The invalidity of categories based on phenotypic traits. In a population, phenotypic traits vary, and not all members of a population are exactly the same phenotypically.
- The range of phenotypic traits of a population may change without genetic changes.
- An example of this is listed below:

Cranial Differences

- The size of the cranium or other parts of the body may be related to the diet of the individual and group. For example, changes in skull form and height are found among children of European immigrants when compared to their parents.
- Shape of the cranium may also be due to cultural practices indicating status and group membership, such as occurred with pre-Hispanic Maya, Inca, and other indigenous groups of Central and South America (see Boada Rivas 1987).

Possible Reasons for Racism

- To establish an ascribed hierarchy in a society not based on kinship but perceive themselves as being different from the person or group being categorized on perceived physical characteristics.
- The need to differentiate group membership.
- Why? Resource limitation. Racism is a means of restricting access to resources.

FIGURE 7.1. Deliberate deformation of the skull with the band shown in the photograph used to induce the shape change. Referred to as "Toulouse deformity." Photographer and date unknown. Restoration and digitization by Didier Descouens; created on June 7, 2013. *Copyright © Didier Descouens (CC BY-SA 3.0) at http://commons.wikimedia.org/ wiki/File:%C2%AB_d%C3%A9formation_ toulousaine_%C2%BB_MHNT.jpg.*

- It is used to justify, explain, and preserve a group's privileged social position by declaring "the other" (other groups) innately or, in other words, biologically inferior.

Examples of Racism

- Sports and race issues: Culture and the environment define success in sports, not biology.
- Physical activities, including sports, which are influenced by culture, help build phenotype.
- Appropriate sports to play, appropriate behaviors for genders, location of growth, interests, etc., all affect a person's physical abilities.

- Race and IQ: Another form of racist justification. Variation in knowledge is cultural, not biological.
- IQ tests measure economic and social background and education, but nothing else. Some people may be smarter than others, but this cannot be generalized to whole populations.
- How do you measure intelligence? If you base it on formal knowledge that is taught, then the education of a person is being measured, and there is differential access to education.
- In one early study (Klineberg 1951), Native Americans from reservations did poorly on intelligence testing, but with the development of better school systems, their scores improved dramatically.

- Race and racism are social and historical constructions.
- Race is situational: It is based on categorization done by a person or groups who perceive themselves as being different from the person/or group be categorized. It reflects labor, economic, and social relations.
- Race and ethnicity are situational. (The categorizations termed "imagined communities" will be covered later. These change based on the situation of the individual and group.)

Ideologies of Segregation

- U.S. and institutional segregation, race and ethnicity: a product of government policies.
- Examples: apartheid in South Africa and in the U.S. up to the Civil Rights Act of 1964 (see Lyon 1992).

United States Supreme Court Cases Regarding Racism, Segregation, and Civil Rights

- See www.crmvet.org for further information.
- 1896. *Plessy v. Ferguson* ruling that sanctioned "separate but equal" segregation of the races.
- 1954. The Supreme Court rules on the landmark case *Brown v. Board of Education of Topeka, Kansas*, unanimously agreeing that segregation in public schools is unconstitutional.
- 1956. Buses are desegregated in Montgomery, Alabama, after a boycott lead by Reverend Martin Luther King, Jr., lasts a year following Rosa Parks' arrest for not giving up her seat to a white bus rider.
- 1963. Reverend Martin Luther King, Jr., delivers his "I Have a Dream Speech."
- 1963. The 24th Amendment to the Constitution abolishes the poll tax that had occurred in eleven southern states to make it difficult for poor black and white people to vote.
- 1964. President Johnson signs the Civil Rights Act of 1964, which prohibits discrimination of all kinds, based on race, color, religion, or national origin.
- 1965. The Voting Rights Act of 1965 makes literacy tests, taxes, and other hindrances to voter registration illegal.
- 1967. In *Loving v. Virginia*, the Supreme Court rules that prohibiting interracial marriage is unconstitutional. Incidentally, the film *Guess Who's Coming to Dinner* was released six months later (December 1967) and dealt with the subject of interracial marriage and starred Sidney Poitier, Spencer Tracy, Katherine Hepburn, and her niece Katherine Houghton. Directed by Stanley Kramer and written by William Rose.
- 1968. President Johnson signs the Civil Rights Act of 1968, prohibiting discrimination in the sale, rental, and financing of housing.

- 1988. Overriding President Reagan's veto, Congress passes the Civil Rights Restoration Act, which expands the reach of non-discrimination laws within private institutions receiving federal funds.
- 1991. President Bush signs the Civil Rights Act of 1991, strengthening existing civil rights laws and providing for damages in cases of intentional employment discrimination.
- In the most important affirmative action decision since the 1978 *Bakke* case, the Supreme Court (five to four) upholds the University of Michigan Law School's policy, ruling that race can be one of many factors considered by colleges when selecting their students, because it furthers educational benefits that arise from having a diverse student body at the college or university.

Other Issues Related to Race

- Affirmative Action: a set of policies designed, initially, to increase participation of African Americans and other minorities in settings and positions traditionally dominated by privileged whites. Designed to counteract the institutionalized segregationist policies prior to the 1960s against these persons in the United States.

- Accommodation: a form of segregation. Examples: Italian neighborhoods in Boston and New York and Chinatowns.
- Racist ideologies today: ascription based on color or ethnicity.
- Hypodescent: form of descent that automatically places the offspring of a union between members of different groups in the minority group. Common in the U.S.

- The ideology of compromise: one's class/status affects one's racial classification ("money whitens"). Example: Brazil. The category of Indian and Cabôclos. Cabôclos is a term for assimilated indigenous people in Brazil.
- In this case, race can change based on class membership (not found in U.S. where race assignment stays the same regardless of class).

Example of the Races One Can Choose from on the U.S. 2010 Census Form

9. What is Person 1's race? *Mark one or more boxes.*

White

Black, African Am., or Negro

American Indian or Alaska Native – *Print name of enrolled or principal tribe.*

Asian Indian

Chinese

Filipino

Other Asian — *Print race, for example, Hmong, Laotian, Thai, Pakistani, Cambodian, and so on.*

Japanese

Korean

Vietnamese

Native Hawaiian

Guamanian or Chamorro

Samoan

Other Pacific Islander – *Print race, for example, Fijian, Tongan, and so on.*

Some other race – *Print race.*

From http://2010.census.gov/2010census/about/interactive-form.php
See the 2010 Census - About - Explore the 2010 Census Form

- Some models used by states make the existence of racism invisible or irrelevant.
- Examples: The multiplication of cultural categories (achieved categories) and the category of Mestizo (persons of mixed ethnic/indigenous background).

Solutions: The Elimination of Ascribed Categories

- When conflicts occur, individuals have the choice of retreating into more constrained aspects of territoriality in space and time (i.e., reassertion of ethnicity, religious identity, racial identity), or they can embrace notions of the state (i.e., secular or religious) in their dealings with others.

CHAPTER EIGHT

Homo sapiens and Their Relationship to Primates

Human are Primates

- Hominoids (Hominoidea)
- Hominoids are comprised of three families: the Hominidae, the Pongidae, and the Hylobatidae.
- Today, humans are classified as belonging to the family Hominidae, along with chimpanzees and gorillas. The two other families of ape include the Pongidae (orangutans) and the Hylobatidae (gibbons and siamangs).
- The tribe Hominini, or term hominin, now refers to living humans and the fossil remains indicating their line of ancestry.
- The genus, species, and subspecies scientific classification of living humans is *Homo sapiens sapiens.*

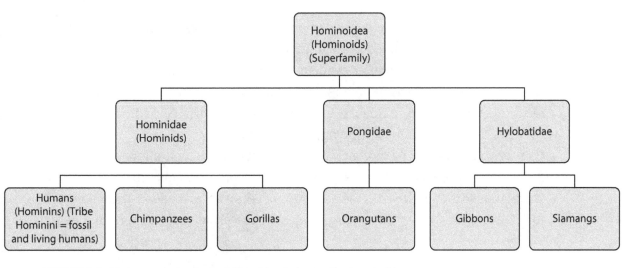

FIGURE 8.1. Phylogeny indicating relationships between the hominoids.

- Humans share a very distant ancestry with other primates. The arrangement of a group of species that share a common ancestor is called a family tree or phylogeny.
- A phylogeny is built based on shared physical characteristics.

Features that Define Primates

- The big toe on the foot is opposable and hands are prehensile
- Nails instead of claws
- Unspecialized olfactory (smelling) apparatus
- Highly developed vision
- Females have small litters; gestation and juvenile periods are longer than in other mammals
- Large brain
- Molars are unspecialized and there is a maximum of two incisors, one canine, three premolars, and three molars on each half of upper and lower jaw

Examples of Behaviors Shared with Other Primates and Ancestors

- Territoriality: "domain" or the extent of land under the control of a particular group.
- Individual and group component
- Spatial and temporal component
- Bases, ranges, and boundaries
- Food comes from many different resources. Generally unspecialized.
- Group cohesion and dispersion based on seasonality and availability of food.
- Food sharing. Part of risk management strategies.
- Mating practices: Competition by both males and females. In general, males compete to have numerous mates, whereas females compete for resources to raise offspring. Key to reproductive success of the individual and passing on of genes. Linked to reproductive biology in primates.
- Care of young usually by mother who invests heavily in each offspring. The long developmental period for humans to reach maturity appears to have been a characteristic that occurred in the genus *Homo*, even as long ago as potentially 1.8 to 1.6 million years ago with *Homo erectus*. These skeletal remains have a pelvic

ratio of size of mother's birth canal to baby's head that indicates that the infant's brain and body could not have been close to maturity when it was born. Males do not care for young when 1) they can use their resources to obtain additional matings or 2) caring for young will not appreciably increase the offspring's fitness.

- Use of tools or technology
- Symbolic behavior leading to the development of language

CHAPTER NINE

The Origins of Our Species

The Pliocene

- The Pliocene is dated 5 million years ago (mya) to 2.2 mya.
- First possible ancestors of *Homo sapiens*.
- Referred to as hominin, a term used to designate the human line after its split from ancestral chimpanzees.
- Hominids now used to refer to fossilized and living humans, chimpanzees, gorillas, and their ancestors.
- *Sahelanthropus tchadensis* is a possible common ancestor to humans and chimps. Remains consisted of a skull dated to 6 mya to 7 mya. Found in Central Africa in Chad's Djurab Desert.

Ardipithecus ramidus

- Oldest known skeleton of a potential human ancestor. Reported on in *Science* in 2009 (for instance, see Gibbons 2009; White et al. 2009).
- Located in Aramis, Ethiopia
- Dated to 4.4 mya. *Ardipithecus* is believed to have lived from 5.8 to 4.4 mya.
- Remains include the skull, teeth, pelvis, hands, and feet of a female individual
- Reveals an "intermediate" form of upright walking or bipedalism
- Opposable toe

- Flexible hands
- Blades of the pelvis are broad indicating upright posture
- Canines are intermediate between chimpanzees and humans
- From other plant and animal remains dated to the same time period, researchers conclude that "Ardi" lived in a woodland, climbing among hackberry, fig, and palm trees and coexisting with monkeys, kudu antelopes, and peafowl. Doves and parrots flew overhead.
- All these creatures prefer woodlands, not the open, grassy terrain often conjectured as the habitat for our ancestors.

The Pleistocene

- The Pleistocene is divided into:
- Lower (1.64 mya–900,000 years ago)
- Middle (900,000–130,000 years ago)
- Upper (130,000–12,000 years ago)
- The middle Pleistocene is characterized by the massive expansion of continental glaciers.
- As *Homo sapiens,* we originated around 130,000 years ago in the African savanna tropics.

Australopithecines

- *Australopithecus afarensis*
- Best known from examples of skeletons found at Hadar in Northeastern Ethiopia and the Awash Basin in Ethiopia
- The most famous example is popularly known as "Lucy," the skeletal remains of a female of 3.2 mya

Characteristics of Australopithecus afarensis:

- Cranium is apelike with small endocranial volume of 404 cubic centimeters (cm^3), less than a pint
- Cranium is flared at the bottom, known as pneumatized
- Front of face below the nose is pushed out, known as subnasal prognathism

- Dentition has evidence of diastema, or gap between the canine and neighboring incisor to allow for larger canines
- Shape of pelvis is similar to humans indicating *A. afarensis* stood upright or was bipedal, walking on two feet
- Sexual dimorphism in body size is present

Explanation for Evolution of Bipedality

- Walking on two legs is an efficient form of locomotion on the ground.
- Erect posture allowed hominin to remain cool in warm weather.
- Bipedal locomotion keeps the hands free to carry things.
- Bipedal posture allows for efficient harvesting of fruits from small trees.

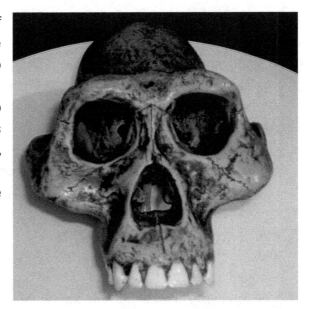

FIGURE 9.1. Australopithecus afarensis skull reconstruction. Displayed at the Museum of Man in San Diego, California. Photograph by Durova; created on December 4, 2007.

Copyright © Durova (CC BY-SA 4.0) at http://commons.wikimedia.org/wiki/File:Australopithecusafarensis_reconstruction.jpg.

Wait! How Do We Know These Skeletal and Other Remains Date to These Time Periods?

Measuring Time

- Relative dating: the idea that something is older (or younger) relative to something else and depends on the ordering of artifacts, deposits, societies, and events into sequences, earlier before later.
- Absolute dating: absolute age in years before the present through the use of various techniques developed for dating. Sometimes called chronometric dating.

Relative Dating Methods

- Stratigraphy: the study of stratification or the laying down or deposition of strata or layers (or deposits), one above the other.
- Law of superposition: those strata laid down first will be older than overlying strata.
- Association: when two objects are found related within the same archaeological deposit, indicating that they became buried at the same time.

Typological Sequences
- Arrangement of artifacts, buildings, etc. into rough chronological sequences.
- Uses the artifacts' specific attributes of material, shape, and decoration (i.e., ceramics).
- Several artifacts with the same attributes are one type. Several types can then be arranged into a chronological sequence.

Absolute Dating Methods

- Absolute dating methods depend on the existence of regular time-dependent processes.
- Examples of absolute dating methods: calendars and historical chronologies and annual cycles, such as varves and tree rings.

Radioactive Clocks
- The principle of radioactive decay:
- Most elements occur in more than one isotopic form.
- Through time, as an object decays, these isotopes change ratios.
- The time taken for half of the atoms of a radioactive isotope to decay is called its half-life.
- The half-life is dependent on the radioactive isotope under study (i.e., 14C has a half-life of 5,730 years, while 238U has a half-life of 4.5 billion years.).
- This takes place at a constant rate and can be measured to give a good estimate of the time of death, inclusion in the archaeological record, or decay of an object.
- Examples of absolute dating methods utilizing the concepts involved in radioactive clocks:

Radiocarbon Dating

- In 1949 Willard Libby, an American chemist working at the University of Chicago, published the first radiocarbon dates.
- Carbon has three isotopes: 12C, 13C, and 14C with 98.9% being 12C, 1.1% being 13C, and only one atom in a billion atoms of carbon being 14C.
- 14C (radiocarbon) is formed in the upper atmosphere by cosmic rays bombarding nitrogen (14N). It is unstable, because it has eight neutrons in the nucleus instead of the usual six (12C). It decays back to 14N after an organism has died and has stopped absorbing 14C through carbon dioxide uptake during photosynthesis and herbivorous and carnivorous consumption.
- The decay is at a steady rate with a half-life of 5,730 years.
- This ratio can be measured to determine the time at which the decay began (time of deposition in the archaeological record, time of death). In essence, one is counting the beta particles that are released from a sample based on the 14C left in it.
- The accurate measurement of 14C activity of a sample can be affected by counting errors, background cosmic radiation, and other factors.
- Therefore, radiocarbon dates are invariably accompanied by an estimate of the probable error, notated as the ± term (standard deviation) given with every radiocarbon date (i.e., 3,700 ± 100 Before Present (BP) or a 68% probability—two in three chance—that the correct age estimate in radiocarbon years lies between 3,800 and 3,600 BP).
- Calibration programs and curves can be obtained from the radiocarbon website at www.radiocarbon.org.

Potassium-Argon (K-Ar)(and Argon-Argon) Dating

- Used to date rocks hundreds or even a few billion years old and, in effect, are geological dates for rock samples.
- One of the most appropriate techniques for dating early human and primate (hominin and hominid) sites in Eastern Africa, which can be up to 5 million years old, including at Olduvai Gorge in Tanzania and Hadar in Ethiopia with remains of Australopithecines, *Homo habilis*, and *Homo erectus*.
- Potassium-argon dating, like radiocarbon dating, is based on the principle of radioactive decay.
- Limiting factors: it can only date sites buried by volcanic rock that are generally not more recent than 100,000 years old, and it is rarely possible to achieve an accuracy better than ± 10% (i.e., 1 million years ± 100,000,000 years).

Uranium-Series Dating

- Based on the radioactive decay of isotopes of uranium.
- Is particularly useful for the period 500,000–50,000 years ago, which falls outside of the time range of radiocarbon dating.
- Uses: in Europe where potassium-argon dating cannot be conducted due to a lack of volcanic rock and uranium-series dating can determine the age of hominid sites, such as Neanderthal remains.
- Limiting factors: the dating method is often used on cave sites that are known to be difficult to excavate and to determine correct stratigraphy of layers. Artifacts, human skeletal remains, and teeth trapped in these travertine layers can, thus, be dated with caution.

Fission-Track Dating

- Based on the spontaneous fission of an isotope of uranium (238U) present in a wide range of rocks and minerals, obsidian and other volcanic glasses, glassy meteorites (tektites), manufactured glasses, and mineral inclusions in pottery.
- Produces useful dates from suitable rocks that contain or are adjacent to those containing archaeological evidence. Useful for early Paleolithic sites and can verify the potassium-argon method.
- Limiting factors: usefulness to samples that are older than roughly 300,000 years old. However the method has been used to date ceramics and obsidian of less than 2,000 years.

Thermoluminescence (TL) Dating (a non-radioactive method of dating)

- Two advantages over radiocarbon dating: it can date pottery, one of the most abundant artifacts of humans, and it can date inorganic materials (such as flints) beyond 50,000 years, the limit for 14C dating.
- Poorer precision than radiocarbon dating.
- Possible to empty what is called electron traps by the application of heat.
- TL dating, therefore, may be performed on minerals, which have had their electron counts set to zero by exposure to high temperatures prior to burial.
- Limiting factors: one must test the surrounding soil to determine the amount of radioactivity in the soil context.

Electron Spin Resonance (ESR) Dating

- ESR is less sensitive than TL but is suitable for materials that decompose when heated.
- Most successful in dating tooth enamel, which has zero electrons when first formed but begins to accumulate these once the tooth is buried and exposed to natural radiation.

- Limiting factors include the age range of ESR dating, since the stability of the trapped electrons begins to deteriorate.
- The accuracy of the method is also compromised by the need to model uranium uptake.
- Not good for dating bone, and often produces under-estimations of age.

Other Calibrated Relative Methods

- Obsidian Hydration: Dating procedure based on the principle that when obsidian is fractured, it begins to absorb water from its surroundings and forms a hydration layer that can be measured.
- Amino-Acid Racemization: Dating method used to date bone (only 10 grams of human or animal bone) up to about 100,000 years old.
- Cation-Ratios and Dating of Rock Art: Dating method depends on the principle that the cations of certain elements (i.e., charged atoms of elements that combine with oxide and hydroxide ions of opposite charge to form stable compounds) are more soluble than those of certain other elements. They leach out of the varnish that forms on rock surfaces exposed to desert dust and their concentration decreases through time. One could then simply measure the ratio of these mobile cations (like potassium [K] and calcium [Ca]), to the more stable cations of titanium (Ti). Limiting factors: a lack of an absolute decay rate and various forms of contamination may affect these ratios.
- Chlorine-36 Dating: Dating of rock art that depends on the accumulation of nucleotides at and near the surface of the rock when it is exposed to cosmic radiation. The amount of 36Cl close to the surface exposure is compared to the unexposed area. When exposure has been over a long time, the amount of 36Cl concentration is higher. Limiting factors: it does not give an actual date of the engraving but simply indicates the amount of time of exposure of the rock surface.
- Archaeomagnetic Dating: Dating of objects that have undergone heating (for instance clay baked to 650 to 700 degrees Celsius and not reheated) so that iron particles in their structures align with the earth's magnetic direction and intensity at the time of firing. This alignment can be calibrated against the known variation through time in magnetic direction so that the object can be dated. Limiting factors: regional variations with the global magnetic field mean that a separate master sequence must be made for each region, and only a few currently exist (i.e., Britain and the American Southwest).

The Lower Pleistocene (1.64 MYA to 900,000 Years Ago): Early Homo Remains

Homo habilis

- *Homo habilis* or handy man
- Remains date from 1.6 to 1.9 mya
- Locations of finds include Olduvai Gorge in Tanzania, East Africa
- Another important find is OH62 dating to 1.8 mya. Skeletal remains look very similar to Lucy in anatomy with long arms and legs, possibly reflecting use of trees for refuge.
- Small in size

Characteristics of Homo habilis:
- Brain size is larger than in Australopithecines
- Teeth are smaller and dentition more parabolic
- Skulls are more rounded; the face is smaller, and less protrusion of the face is evident
- Some of the earliest evidence of use of tools are associated with these remains (see Boyd and Silk 2015, 2000)
- Oldowan pebble tools
- Use of choppers from cores and stone flakes
- Recovered from Olduvai Gorge, Tanzania, dated to 1.8 mya
- Older tools recovered from Ethiopia, Congo, and Malawi dated to 2.6 to 2.0 mya
- Associated with a new species of hominin, *Australopithecus garhi,* with skeletal remains recovered in Ethiopia

Homo erectus

- Remains date to 1.6 to 1.8 mya
- Finds at Lake Turkana, Kenya, in East Africa are quite different from *H. habilis* and modern humans

Characteristics of Homo erectus:
- Skulls of *Homo erectus* retain many of the characteristics of earlier hominins:
- Browridges

- A skull that narrows markedly behind the eyes
- A receding forehead
- A flattened skull relative to modern humans
- A broad, flat face
- No chin
- Derived characteristics like modern humans:
- A smaller, less prognathic face
- A smaller, shorter ramus of the mandible (part of lower jaw)
- Smaller teeth
- Vestibular (inner ear) system similar to modern humans
- Tall.
- Pelvic ratio of size of mother's birth canal to baby's head same as in modern humans, leading to the conclusion that children were born before full brain development and needed extended parental care
- Acheulean tool technology
- Standardized hand axes used in butchery
- Associated to *Homo erectus*
- Dated mainly to the Lower Pleistocene (1.64 mya to 900,000 years ago) and into the middle of the Middle Pleistocene (900,000 to 300,000 years ago)
- This tool technology remained in use for almost 1 million years

The Middle Pleistocene: Europe (900,000 to 130,000 Years Ago)

Homo erectus *and Archaic* Homo sapiens

- *Homo erectus* had spread throughout temperate Eurasia
- Archaic *Homo sapiens* appear to have coexisted in Eastern Asia with *Homo erectus*
- Early evidence of Archaic *Homo sapiens* is from Trinchera Dolina in the Sierra de Atapuerca (Spain)
- Dates between 800,000 and 500,000 years ago
- 80 individuals. Very fragmented remains.
- *Homo erectus* remains also found in China and Java
- Sima de los Huesos (Spain) also provides evidence of changes from *Homo erectus* to *Homo sapiens*, and, probably, to Neanderthals

- Nearderthals dominate Europe from 130,000 to 30,000 years ago
- Neanderthal or Neandertal means "people of the Neander valley" ("tall" is valley) in German
- Technologies associated to Neandertals include the use of wooden throwing spears. Evidence comes from Germany and is related to the hunting of horses.
- Variation in tool types increases. Hand axes are replaced by retouched large flakes which are primary flakes struck from a pebble or core with the edges of the flakes revealing further removal of tiny secondary flakes.

CHAPTER TEN

The Evolution of *Homo sapiens:* The Last 100,000 Years

- As indicated the Pleistocene is divided into:
- Lower (1.64 mya–900,000 years ago)
- Middle (900,000–130,000 years ago)
- Upper (130,000–12,000 years ago). Also broken down into Paleolithic time periods.
- Paleolithic: of the Stone Age, marked by the use of stone implements.
- Warmer interglacial period occurred between 130,000 and 75,000 years ago. The *Würm* glacial period occurred from 75,000 to 12,000 years ago (BP).

Middle to Upper Pleistocene Hominins: Neanderthals and Others

- Along with *Homo erectus, Homo sapiens* expanded over Europe and the Near East
- Early sites with remains of *Homo erectus* outside of Africa include:
- Dmanisi site in the former Soviet Republic of Georgia. One fairly complete skull, one large mandible, and two partial skulls. Dated 1.7 to 1.77 mya.
- Discovered in 1891 near Trinil on the island of Java, a skull and thigh bone date from 700,000 years ago to, possibly, as much as 1.6 mya. Referred to as "Java Man."
- The largest group of *Homo erectus* remains comes from Zhoukoudian Cave in China. Tools, hearths, animal bones, and more than 40 hominins, including five skulls, were recovered. Dated to 670,000 to 410,000 BP. Previously referred to as "Peking Man."

- Zhoukoudian Cave or Choukoutien Cave is outside of Peking and was opened in 1927 by Davidson Black from Canada. The excavation eventually reached 80 feet (ft) below the ground surface, and that is where he found fossils of "Peking Man," later identified as *Homo erectus* (Johanson and Edey 1981, 34–35).

- Other Middle Pleistocene remains associated to the genus *Homo*:
- *Homo naledi*. Site: Rising Star Cave System, Gauteng Province, South Africa. At least 15 individuals and over 1,550 specimens recovered from the cave. Possible dates include 2 mya to 912,000 B. P. (Berger et al. 2015).
- *Homo antecessor*. Site: Gran Dolina in the Atapuerca Mountains of Spain. Dated to 780,000 BP.
- *Homo heidelbergensis*. Site: Mauer near Heidelberg, Germany. Dated to 500,000 BP. A massive hominin jaw found in 1907, originally referred to as "Heidelberg Man."
- *Homo floresiensis*. Characterized by unusually small anatomical features compared to other examples of *Homo* remains. Site: Flores, an Indonesian island east of Bali. Dated to 95,000 to 13,000 BP.

- As indicated, Neanderthal or Neandertal means "people of the Neander valley" ("tall" is valley) in German. Remains first found in this valley in 1856. Until recently, Neanderthals were thought to be the direct ancestors to *Homo sapiens*. Classified variably as *Homo sapiens neanderthalensis* or *Homo neanderthalensis*. Various remains dated to 130,000 to 28,000 BP.

Possible Models of *Homo sapiens* Evolution

- The multiregional model: although hominin populations were spread out between Africa and Eurasia, enough gene flow (migrations and mating) occurred to keep all of the Middle Pleistocene hominins evolving into one single species, *Homo sapiens*.
- The replacement model: three distinct species are identified for Africa, Western Eurasia, and Eastern Eurasia. In Africa, *Homo ergaster* evolved into *Homo sapiens* about 400,000 years ago and into *Homo erectus* in Asia, while isolated populations in Europe diverged into *Homo neanderthalensis*. If true, the last common ancestor between humans and Neanderthals lived between 550,000 and 600,000 years ago.

Middle/Upper Pleistocene Sites with Remains of Anatomically Modern Humans

- Herto village in Ethiopia. Three skulls missing the lower jaws. Dated to 154,000 to 160,000 BP.
- Also Omo-kibish in Ethiopia. Originally dated to ca. 130,000 BP. Now thought to be 195,000 BP. Numerous remains found.
- Pinnacle Point Cave and Border Cave in South Africa. Dated possibly back to 150,000 BP. Remains of five individuals including an infant of four to six months old buried in a shallow grave.
- Klasies River mouth in South Africa (see Binford 1984). Dates between 134,000 and 74,000 BP.
- Qafzeh and Skhul caves in Israel. Dates to 90,000 years ago.
- Sites with Neanderthal remains in the Middle East include Kebara (110,000 BP), Tabun, and Amud (55,000 to 60,000 BP).

Characteristics of Neanderthals

- Large brain (from 1245 to 1740 cm^3, average around 1520 cm^3). Modern humans is about 1400 cm^3.
- More rounded crania than *Homo erectus*, long and low
- Big faces, large brow ridges, large nose
- Small molars and large front teeth. Fused taurodont root (single broad root). Scratches on front of incisors indicate they may have held meat in teeth while cutting it.
- Robust body, heavily muscled bodies. Weighted about 30% more than modern humans—may be related to the conservation of heat in colder climates.
- Thicker bones
- The crural index is the ratio of the length of the tibia (shin bone) to the length of the femur (thigh bone). It measures the relative limb length and is correlated with environmental temperature.
- The Neanderthal crural index is similar to that of the Lapps, who live above the Arctic Circle, and is given solely as an example of the association between relative limb length and temperature; the Neanderthals had short, stocky limbs (see Stein and Rowe 2000).

Mousterian Technology and Neanderthal Life Ways

- Hunted large game often of the same species. However, there is some questioning of whether this was actually hunting or not. The evidence may indicate that these individuals were possible scavengers, since often only the skull and foot bones of animals are found in the base camp activity areas.
- Lived in base camps located in rock shelters
- Tool technology: Mousterian.
- Probably buried their dead. More preserved skeletons are found. Pollen is found in a burial at Shanidar Cave, Iraq, that may have been a garland of flowers added to the burial.
- Neanderthals die young. Skeletal remains show bone fractures, wounds, gum disease, arthritis (usually did not live past 40 years).

- Upper Paleolithic Subsistence in Europe
- Hunting of: deer, bison, bear, horse, wild sheep, wild goats.

- Upper Paleolithic subsistence in South Africa
- Klasies River
- Harvested: buffalo, bushpigs, capefur seal, shellfish.

The Moderns: Anatomically Modern People

The Upper Paleolithic (ca. 50,000 to 10,000 BP)

- In Europe, modern humans appear at the Cro-Magnon site (30,000 years ago) near Les Eyzies-de-Tayac, Dordogne, France.
- Replacement of Neanderthals
- Modern humans enter Australia around 40,000 years ago (first people to use polished stone tools). Evidence at Lake Mungo.

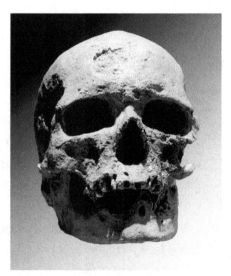

FIGURE 10.1. Cranium recovered from the Cro-Magnon rock shelter (Cro-Magnon 1), curated at the Musée de l'Homme, Paris. Photograph by 120; created April, 2007.
Copyright © 120 (CC BY-SA 3.0) at http://commons.wikimedia.org/wiki/File:Cro-Magnon.jpg.

Characteristics of Modern *Homo sapiens:*

- Small faces with protruding chin. Possible reasons for a chin: mouth not used as a tool as often and may have helped in speech production.
- Rounded skull, possibly assisting in brain development.
- Less robust skeleton (i.e., longer limbs and thinner bones) and may have relied less on strength and more on tools.

Upper Paleolithic Technology: Europe

- Use of blade tools (stone flakes that look like modern knife blades)
- Use of atlatl or spear thrower (14,000 BP)
- Use of the bow and arrow (10,000 BP)
- The Aurignacian tool tradition (35,000 to 27,000 BP)
- The Gravettian tool tradition (27,000 to 21,000 BP)
- The Solutreand tool tradition (21,000 to 16,500 BP)
- The Magdalenian tool tradition (ca. 16,000 to ca. 10,000 BP)

- Use of atlatl or spear-thrower
- More elaborate tool kit
- Wider variety of materials used (bones, antlers, teeth)
- Materials transported large distances
- Made elaborate shelters

Upper Paleolithic Art

- Lascaux cave paintings (France) (12,000 BP)
- Le Chauvet cave paintings (France) (30,000 BP)
- Figurines (ca. 20,000 BP)
- Indicative of symbolic behavior. Symbols possibly used in the differentiation of groups.
- There are also multiple burials and the dead were buried with tools, ornaments, and other objects that may indicate a belief in life after death or group affiliation. At the Siberian site of Mal'ta (15,000 years ago), a child was buried with jewelry, tools, figurines, and a diadem.

Summary of Upper Paleolithic Life Ways of Anatomically Modern *Homo sapiens*

- Lived at higher population levels than Neanderthals
- Lived longer (up to 60 years) than Neanderthals
- Were less likely to suffer from serious injuries or illnesses
- Had more complex forms of shelters and clothing (i.e., used mammoth bones and skins to make shelters, such as at the Gravettian Předmostí Site in the Czech Republic and the sites of Moldova in Russia)
- Lived in egalitarian kin-based bands in which food was shared with no formal political organization

Simplified Ancestry of Humans (*Homo sapiens*)

- *Australopithecus afarensis*. 3.2 mya. East Africa. Bipedal.
- *Australopithicus sediba*. 2.0 mya. South Africa. Combined features of *Australopithecus* and *Homo* species.
- *Homo habilis*. 1.9–1.6 mya. East Africa. Use of tools.
- *Homo erectus*. 1.6 mya–300,000 BP. Africa, Europe, Asia. Larger brain and skeletal sizes.
- Archaic *Homo sapiens*. 800,000-35,000 BP. Africa, Europe, Asia. Various *Homo* species (*H. naledi* [2 mya-912,000 BP], *H. antecessor*, *H. heidelbergensis*, *H. floresiensis*).
- Neanderthals. *Homo neanderthalensis* or *Homo sapiens neanderthalensis*. 130,000–35,000 BP. Europe, Southwestern Asia. Robust features. Expansion of tool types.
- *Homo sapiens sapiens*. 130,000 BP to present. Worldwide. Modern physical characteristics. Symbolic behavior.

PART THREE

Archaeology

Where Food Comes From: Diversification of Subsistence and the Origins of Food Production

Introduction

"Advances in subsistence technologies are a necessary precondition for any significant increase in either the size or the complexity of any society" (Nolan and Lenski 2006, 57).

"Complex societies are those in which hierarchically ordered social components exhibit marked functional differentiation and specialization. The components are therefore functionally interdependent in that no individual or group can fulfill all of the required roles and duties" (Carmichael 1995, 181).

- After the lithic revolution of the Oldowan, the Acheulean hand axe technology was successful for almost 1 million years.
- The invention of pottery was a major technological achievement.
- Pottery was first invented in Japan around 12,000 years ago.
- However, early pottery at ca. 20,000 years ago has recently been reported as recovered from Xianrendong Cave, Jiangxi Province, China (Wu et al. 2012).

- In the Americas, pottery was invented only 7,000 years ago in Northern and Central South America (see Oyuela-Caycedo and Bonzani 2014, 2005; Roosevelt et al. 1991).
- In Northern Africa. 10,000 years ago.
- In the Levant. 8,000 years ago.
- Pottery was important, because it changed the way that humans processed their food for consumption, and it improved health conditions in relation such foods by removing some of the toxins.
- Initially, pottery had a ritual use for serving and fermentation. Later, its function expanded to the cooking of meals.
- Before pottery, most of the food was cooked by direct fire or roasting pits (earth oven features) and heating (fire-cracked) rocks.

FIGURE 11.1. Excavation at San Jacinto 1 in Northern Colombia, illustrating earth oven features and fire-cracked rocks for cooking (Photo by Augusto Oyuela-Caycedo and Renée M. Bonzani) (see Oyuela-Caycedo and Bonzani 2014, 2005).

Augusto Oyuela-Caycedo and Renée M. Bonzani, "Figure 3.3: Example of stratigraphy as recovered at the site of San Jacinto 1, northern Colombia," San Jacinto 1: A Historical Ecological Approach to an Archaic Site in Colombia, pp. 53. Copyright © 2005 by University of Alabama Press. Reprinted with permission.

Origins of Food Production

- The shift from collecting food to food cultivation is also linked to the beginning of the Holocene Period. It began to occur around 10,000 years ago in the Levant (Palestine, Israel, Syria) (Pre-pottery Neolithic period) (Price 2009).
- In Asia, around the same time, as well as in Thailand, China, and Indus River Delta (Pakistan).
- In Turkey, Iraq, and the Zagros Mountains in Iran.
- In the Americas, evidence for early cultigens has also been pushed back to 10,000 to 8,000 BP in Peru and Mexico (Smith 2014, 2011, 2006, 1992, 1987, 1984; Smith and Cowan 2003; Smith and Yarnell 2009).

FIGURE 11.2.
Copyright © 2008 Fir0002, GNU Free Documentation License at: https://commons.wikimedia.org/wiki/File:Sunflower_sky_backdrop.jpg. A copy of the license can be found here: https://en.wikipedia.org/wiki/GNU_Free_Documentation_License.

Why We Domesticated Plants

- Conditions: population pressure, reduced mobility, competition for resources.
- Intensification in terms of the use of space with wild foods that are selected because of the large number of offspring (seeds) and short timing in reproduction.
- Management of risk in relation to dry seasons or winter conditions and predictability in their availability.

Food Production Favored Human Populations to be Able To:

- Live in small villages that have the characteristics of supporting extended families
- Territorial control of land
- Division of labor in terms of gender
- Strong basis in kinship relations

- Storage of resources in relation to seasons of hunger (dry season or winter season)
- The rise of food production seems to correlate with intensification in processing technologies, as well. Example: fermentation and improvement of health conditions.
- Changes in cosmologies. This was the time of the formation of cemeteries as specialized areas.
- The formation of religious cults: mother goddess, bull cults, skull cults (cult of the ancestors).
- The ancient tell of Jericho is an example of sedentism. This site is located near a major spring at the northern end of the Jordan Valley in Southwest Asia. The site, or tell, is a mound of accumulation of 10,000 years of human occupation (Price and Feinman 2008, 219).

Problems with Increased Food Production and Reduction of Mobility

- Increased population growth
- Increased the spread of transmissible diseases
- Decreased the quality of the food (less protein, more carbohydrates and sugars)
- Warfare
- Economic inequality between groups and hereditary social inequality

Which Plants Were Domesticated

- Americas: tomatoes, potatoes, beans, peanuts, manioc, peppers, squash, quinoa.
- Southeast Asia: rice, millet, taro, yam, banana, oranges, coconut, cucumbers.
- Southwest Asia: emmer wheat, einkorn wheat, lentils, chickpea, barley.
- Africa: millet, African rice, sorghum.
- Which domesticated plants are missing from the list from the Americas? (See Bonzani et al. 2007; Bonzani and Oyuela-Caycedo 2006; Staller et al. 2006 for examples.)
- The adoption of agriculture is related to the needs of the local populations. Some societies remained as hunter-gatherers even up to present day.
- Major dispersion of family languages seems to be related to the expansion of food production technologies and migration of food producers. Example: Indo-European proto-language (Bellwood 2013, 2005).

Domestication of animals

- Husbandry or domestication of animals were activities that occurred after the domestication of plants.
- Domestication of animals allowed humans to colonize and use difficult environments, such as the Sahara-sahel, where agriculture is very limited. It also allowed for the development of technologies, such as horse-drawn vehicles.

Conclusions

- The origins of food production of both plants and animals was a continual process.
- It involved the purposeful cultivation of plants and herding of animals but also included the reduction in the mobility of groups (increased sedentism) and the invention of new technologies, like groundstone lithics and ceramics.
- Once this process was underway, it laid the foundation for a series of human behavioral changes, eventually leading to the development of complex societies.

CHAPTER TWELVE

The Nature and Aims of Archaeology

- Archaeology as anthropology
- Archaeology as history
- Archaeology as science
- The scope of archaeology
- See Browman and Williams 2002; Trigger 2006; Willey and Sabloff 1980.

The History of Archaeology

The Speculative Phase: Eighteenth to Nineteenth Centuries

- The first excavations: Pompeii in Italy and Huaca de Tantalluc on the coast of Peru.
- Pompeii was covered in volcanic ash by the eruption of Mount Vesuvius in AD 79, which allowed for the preservation of the town (see Grant 1979).
- Preserved portraits, such as that of a magistrate and his wife as part of a wall decoration in a Pompeian house, reveal the real-life aspect of archaeological research. (Mural painting, 22.875 inches by 20 5 inches. Probable portrait of Terentius Neo and his wife. Naples, National Archaeological Museum, Grant 1979, 83).
- Plaster casts of victims of the volcanic eruption were discovered at Pompeii by Giuseppe Fiorelli in 1864 (Grant 1979, 80, 83).
- Thomas Jefferson (1743–1826) is credited with conducting the first scientific excavation in the history of archaeology.

- In 1784, he dug a trench or section across a burial mound on his property in Virginia.
- This marks the end of the Speculative Period.

The Beginning of Modern Archaeology

- Research questions:
- The antiquity of humanity
- John Lubbock (1834–1913). Publications: *Prehistoric Times as Illustrated by Ancient Remains, and the Manners and Customs of Modern Savages* (1865) and *The Origins of Civilization and the Primitive Condition of Man* (1889).
- Charles Lyell (1797–1875). Publication: *Principles of Geology* (1833).
- Lyell introduced the concept of uniformitarianism: geologically ancient conditions were the same as those occurring today.
- The Theory of Evolution by Natural Selection formulated by Charles Darwin and A. R. Wallace. Charles Darwin published *On The Origins of Species by Means of Natural Selection* (1859).

- The three-age system: Stone Age, Bronze Age, and Iron Age.

> **Table 12.1 The Three Age System in European Antiquity**
> Stone Age: 3.4 mya – 4,500 B.C. to 2,000 B.C.
> Bronze Age (copper-tin) in Europe: 3,000 B.C. -1,200 B.C.
> [Chalcolithic = beginning of this period with pure copper]
> Iron Age in Europe: 1,200 B.C. – A.D. 400.

- The three-age system was refined by Christian J. Thomsen (1788–1865). Book: *Ledetraad til Nordisk Oldkundskab* (Guide to Northern Antiquity) (1836), published in English in 1848.
- The method: typology: the arrangement of artifacts in chronological or developmental sequence.
- General Augustus Pitt-Rivers (1827–1900) (British scholar, after 1859) viewed archaeology as an extension of anthropology.
- The use of ethnography and archaeology.
- Lewis Henry Morgan (1818–1881). Publication: *Ancient Society* (1877). Stages of savagery, barbarism, and civilization. Used the concept of evolution (gradual change through time) to explain the development of societies.

The Discovering of the Early Civilizations

- Napoleon's expedition to Egypt (1798–1801). Collective works published between 1809 and 1822 in *Description de l'Egypte* (see Coulston Gillispie and Dewachter 1987).
- Francois Champollion (1790–1832). The Rosetta Stone is inscribed with identical texts written in Egyptian hieroglyphics, Coptic, and Greek. Champollion deciphered the Egyptian hieroglyphics in 1822.
- Heinrich Schliemann (1822–1890): Schliemann was a German banker in search of the ancient city of Troy. The site was identified at Hissarlik, Western Turkey in the 1870s and 1880s. "Homer's troy."
- The walls of Troy and the south-east gate are depicted in Schliemann's book on Troy (Schliemann 1976 [1884], 74).
- Schielmann (1976 [1881]) also provides a map of the location of Trojas and a plan of Troy by Emile Burnouf from 1879.
- John Lloyd Stephens (1805–1852)(writer and explorer) and Frederick Catherwood (1799–1854)(artist and architect): *Incidents of travel in Yucatán* (1845 [1973]). Travels in this area in the early 1840s revealed the ruined cities of the ancient Maya (see http://www.smith.edu/libraries/libs/rarebook/exhibitions/catherwood/index.htm for an online exhibit at Smith College of the artist's rendering of the Mayan ruins).

FIGURE 12.1. Photo of the Rosetta Stone, currently in the British Museum in London. Photograph by Hans Hillewaert; created November 21, 2007.
Copyright © Hans Hillewaert (CC BY-SA 4.0) at http://en.wikipedia.org/wiki/File:Rosetta_Stone.JPG.

The Development of Field Techniques

- William Flinders Petrie (1853–1942)(Egypt), Max Uhle (1856–1944)(Bolivia, Ecuador, Peru), Sir Mortimer Wheeler (1890–1976)(Britain, India, Pakistan), Alfred Kidder (1885–1963)(Maya and Southwest U.S.).

- Kidder's "blueprint" for regional strategy:
  1. Reconnaissance
  2. Selection for criteria for ranking the remains of sites chronologically
  3. Seriation into a probable sequence
  4. Stratigraphic excavation
  5. More detailed regional survey and dating

Archaeology of the Twentieth Century

Historical or Cultural Particularism

- Concern with chronology, typology, and the history of particular societies

The New Archaeology: Processual Archaeology

- Lewis Binford (1931–2011). Publications: *In Pursuit of the Past* (1988), *Debating Archaeology* (1989), *Constructing Frames of Reference: An Analytical Method for Archaeological Theory Building Using Ethnographic and Environmental Data* (2001).
- Kent Flannery (1934–Present). Publications: *Guila Naquitz: Archaic Foraging and Early Agriculture in Oaxaca, Mexico* (1986).

Postprocessual Archaeology

- Attempts to include the symbolic or cognitive aspects of early societies into the aspects of research.
- Ian Hodder (1948–Present). Publications: Editor of *Symbolic and Structural Archaeology* (1982), *Reading the Past: Current Approaches to Interpretation in Archaeology* (1986), editor of *Archaeological Theory Today* (2002).

Processual Archaeology: Key Concepts

- The key concepts found in processual archaeology are discussed in Renfrew and Bahn (2000: 39) and outlined below .
  1. The nature of archaeology should be explanatory and not just descriptive. Archaeology's role is to explain past change, not to simply reconstruct the past.

2. Explanation in archaeology should focus on culture process and not culture history. Scientific methods should be used to analyze cultural processes and how changes in economic and social systems take place.

3. The reasoning in archaeology should be deductive and not inductive. The formulation of hypotheses and models and their testing should occur in that sequence and not the other way around whereby one excavates and then tries to fit everything together without a testable hypothesis.

4. Validation in archaeology should come from testing hypotheses and not be based only on the authority or standing of a researcher.

5. The research focus of archaeology should be on the project design and not just on accumulating data. The research should be designed to answer specific questions with the logistics of the excavation project in mind.

6. The choice of approach in archaeology should be quantitative and not just qualitative. Quantitative data can be utilized in statistical procedures to help to interpret the data collected, whereas qualitative approaches often focused just on descriptions of artifacts and/or monuments, for instance.

7. The scope of archaeology should be viewed through optimism and not pessimism. The point of view should be that archaeologists can tackle hard problems involving the reconstruction of social organizations and cognitive systems.

Interpretive or Post-Processual Archaeologies

- The following definitions of interpretive or post-processual archaeologies come from Renfrew and Bahn (2000, 42-43).

    1. Neo-marxist element: archaeologists should not only describe the past but use such insights to try to change the world.

    2. Post-positivist approach: procedures of scientific method are an integral part of systems of domination whereby capitalism exerts its domination or hegemony.

    3. Phenomenological approach: stresses the personal experience of the individual or actor and how he/she encounters the material world and how this shapes our understanding of the world (both individuals in the past and the archaeologists/interpreters).

    4. Praxis approach: stresses the central role of the human agent or actor in the primary significance of human actions or action (praxis) in shaping social realities, experience, and structures.

FIGURE 12.2. Example of megalithic construction. Dólmen da Aboboreira in Baião, Portugal (1982). Photograph by António Miguel de Campos; created February 16, 2006.

Antonio Miguel de Campos, "Megalithic Construction," http://commons.wikimedia.org/ wiki/File:Antadaaboboreira.jpg. Copyright in the Public Domain.

5. Hermeneutic (or interpretive) approach: rejects attempts at generalizations. Emphasis is placed on the uniqueness of each society and culture and the need to study the full context of each of these.

- Overall, identifying and understanding the actions and thoughts of individuals in the past is the goal (also known as cognitive archaeology). Methods try to analyze the symbolic and thought or cognitive aspects of human endeavors/behaviors.

Example: Explaining the European Megaliths

- Various interpretations are often given to explain archaeological sites. An example of this occurrence includes that for the European megaliths, as is given in Renfrew and Bahn (2004).
- Megalithic monuments are prehistoric structures built of large stones, such as dolmens or megalithic tombs. The stones are arranged to form a single chamber, buried under an earthen mound with a single entrance.
- Generally, megalithic monuments were built between 6,000 and 4,000 years ago in Europe during the Neolithic and Bronze Ages.
- Migrationist and diffusionist explanation: diffused from a single people who migrated to Western Europe probably from Crete (megaliths from Crete date after Western European examples).
- Functional-processual explanation: each communal tomb served as a focal point for a dispersed community and acted to legitimize the group's claim to ancestral territories.
- Neo-Marxist explanation: the rituals associated to the megaliths legitimized the inequalities within a society. The tombs and rituals made the established order seem normal or natural.
- Goals include developing an insight into the meaning that the tomb held in a specific context for those who built it and an attempt to develop general cultural patterns.
- The processual and post-processual explanations are not mutually exclusive. Both can help to understand past human lifeways and behaviors.

CHAPTER THIRTEEN

The Archaeological Evidence

Basic Evidence

- The definitions presented in this chapter can be found in any basic introductory archaeology text but specifically came from Renfrew and Bahn (2012, 2004, 2000).
- Artifacts: objects used, modified, or made by people (i.e., lithics, ceramics and metal objects).
- Organic remains: carbon-based objects utilized by humans in the past (i.e., faunal and botanical remains).
- Environmental remains: environmental indicators of past human behavior (i.e., soils and sediments).
- Ecofacts: organic and environmental remains indicative of past human behavior.
- Features: a non-portable artifact; an association of artifacts, ecofacts and environmental variables localized in the landscape (i.e., hearths, postholes, architectural remains).
- Sites: a distinctive spatial clustering of artifacts, features, organic, and environmental remains—the residue of human activity (i.e., lithic scatters, base camps, villages, cities).
- Regions: the area of a group of sites and their surrounding landscapes.

The Importance of Context

- Matrix: the material surrounding an artifact, usually some sort of sediment, like clay, gravel, or sand.
- Provenience: vertical and horizontal location within the matrix (i.e., stratigraphy [see Figure 13.1 and Table 13.1] and horizontal coordinates [see Figure 13.2]).
- Association: occurrence together with other artifactual/ecofactual remains.

FIGURE 13.1. Example of stratigraphy as recovered at the site of San Jacinto 1 in Northern Colombia. Photo by Augusto Oyuela-Caycedo and Renée M. Bonzani (Oyuela-Caycedo and Bonzani 2014, 2005).
Augusto Oyuela-Caycedo and Renée M. Bonzani, "Examples of stratigraphy," Table 1.1 from San Jacinto 1: A Historical Ecological Approach to an Archaic Site in Colombia, pp. 6.

Table 13.1 Radiocarbon Dates from Strata 9 through 20 at San Jacinto 1 (uncalibrated) as Illustrated in Figure 13.1.

Stratum	Feature	Sample no.	Material	Dates BP	δ 13C/12C
10	31	GX-20353	charcoal	5300 ± 75	-28.4
10	15	GX-20352	charcoal	5315 ± 80	-27.4
10	45	GX-20354	charcoal	5325 ± 80	-25.0*
10	57	Beta-77407	charcoal	5330 ± 80	-25.0*
10	53	Beta-77405	charcoal	5510 ± 70	-28.5
12	151	GX-20355	charcoal	5530 ± 80	-25.0*
12	profile	Pitt-0154	charcoal	5665 ± 75	-25.0*
12	profile	Beta-20352	charcoal	5700 ± 430	-25.0*
16?	profile	Pitt-0155	charcoal	5940 ± 60	-25.0*
20	AMS	Beta-183290	charcoal	5400 ± 40	-26.1
20	AMS	Beta-183291	charcoal	5190 ± 40	-25.3
20	AMS	Arizona-AA57882	charcoal	5208 ± 28	-23.6

* Calculated relative to the PDB-1 international standard.

- Each unit is 1 meter [m] by 1 m.
- Each unit has a provenience, including a north and east coordinate and an elevation determined by the depth below ground surface.
- Primary context: the original context, location, or association of material that occurred when the site was utilized and abandoned (i.e., Tutankhamen's tomb in the Valley of the Kings [see Carter 1972 for original photos from this outstanding archaeological discovery]).
- Secondary context: the context that results from disturbances after site abandonment (i.e., looters, previous excavations, plowing, and rodent burrows).

FIGURE 13.2. Example of recording horizontal provenience using a checkerboard grid or the Wheeler box-grid, as utilized for excavations at San Jacinto 1 in Northern Colombia. Photo by Augusto Oyuela-Caycedo and Renée M. Bonzani (Oyuela-Caycedo and Bonzani 2014, 2005).

Formation Processes

Cultural Formation Processes of Artifacts

How People Affect What Survives in the Archaeological Record

- Human behavior:
  1. Acquisition of the raw material
  2. Manufacture
  3. Use
  4. Disposal

- Deliberate burial of objects or the dead.
- Hoards: objects deliberately buried with the intention of returning later to claim them.
- Burial of the dead: graves, mounds, and pyramids with associated grave goods.
- Examples: funerary urns excavated at the top of mounds found at the nonagricultural chiefdoms of Marajó Island at the mouth of the Amazon River (Schaan 2008).

- Human destruction of the archaeological record (i.e., secondary burials or deliberate destruction of sites).

Natural Formation Processes

How Nature Affects What Survives in the Archaeological Record

- Taphonomy: the study of processes that have affected organic materials, such as bone, after death; it also involves the microscopic analysis of tooth marks or cut marks to assess the effects of butchery or scavenging activities.

Inorganic Materials Usually Survive Better than Organic Materials
- Stone tools survive extraordinarily well with some over 2 million years old.
- Fired clay, such as pottery and fired bricks or adobe, is nearly indestructible if well fired.

- *Homo habilis*, or handy man.
- Remains date from 1.6 to 1.9 mya.
- Locations of finds include Olduvai Gorge in Tanzania, East Africa.

- The invention of pottery was a major technological achievement.
- Example of early pottery invented in Japan around 12,000 years ago.
- Pottery fragment from San Jacinto 1, Colombia dated from ca. 6,000 to 5,200 BP.

- Metals such as gold, silver, and lead survive well.
- Copper and bronze are attacked by acid soils and can become oxidized, leaving only a green stain.
- Electrolysis can be utilized to clean objects coated with sea salts. This procedure involves placing the object in a chemical solution and passing a weak current between it and a metal grill.
- The Ardagh chalice appears to have been deposited in a field in Ireland by Viking raiders (Duane 1996).
- Of note, the earliest evidence of metal use in North America is for copper.
- Copper spear points were recovered from the Archaic Renshaw and South Fowl Lake sites near Lake Superior in Ontario.

- Copper-preserved organic material, in association with these points, was dated to between 5,000 and 5,300 BP for the material from the Renshaw site and ca. 6,800 BP for materials from the South Fowl Lake site, Anderson point. In archaeology BP indicates years before the present, or years before 1950 when radiocarbon dating was invented (Renfrew and Bahn 2000: 139).
- The harpoon point and cordage in place were recovered from the Renshaw site, and this association allowed for the cordage and copper point to be dated (Beukens et al. 1992).

Organic Materials
- Survival is determined largely by the following:
- Matrix: surrounding material (i.e., organic material sealed by mud in swamps in anaerobic conditions will survive, such as at the Windover Site in Florida).
- Climate: local environmental conditions.
- Variations in humidity or highly humid conditions, such as tropical forests destroy organic remains.
- Caves and rock shelters generally have more stable environments, and preservation is improved.
- Temperature and precipitation variations as found in temperate climates help to accelerate decay.

- Natural disasters sometimes preserve sites and organic remains (i.e., Pompeii in Italy).

Preservation of Organic Materials
- Dry environments: great aridity or dryness prevents decay (i.e., desiccated corn cob remains from Bat's Cave in New Mexico).

- Genotypic and phenotypic changes from the earliest recovered small corn cobs (about 2 centimeters [cm]) to corn cobs over 12 cm in length may have taken less than 6,000 years.
- Example: Bat Cave, New Mexico (earliest cobs date ca. 2300 BC) (Mangelsdorf 1974).
- Example: carbonized corn kernels. Carbonized botanical remains as opposed to desiccated remains are usually recovered from more humid environments since the carbonization process can preserve the structure of the botanical remains

that would have otherwise decayed in the more humid environments (Pearsall 2000).

- Cold environments: frozen conditions can stop degeneration for years (i.e., 5,300 year old Iceman preserved in the Alps on the border of Italy and Austria).
- The Iceman is noted to be the earliest fully preserved human, as found in 1991, emerging from the melting ice (Renfrew and Bahn 2000).
- Waterlogged environments: wetland sites found in lakes, swamps, marshes, fens, and peat bogs (i.e., Windover Site in Florida, see Doran [2002] for examples of materials recovered in a preserved state due to the waterlogged matrix of the site).

CHAPTER FOURTEEN

Characteristics of Complex Societies:
Case Study on Mesoamerican Archaeology Classic to Post-Classic Periods

Introduction

- Cultural Evolution: Mesoamerica
- Paleoindian Period (35000/14000–8000 BC)
- Archaic Period (8000–2000 BC)
- Preclassic or Formative Period (ca. 2000 BC–AD 300)
- Classic Period (AD 300–900)
- Postclassic Period (AD 900–1521)

- The following information is derived from Price and Feinman (2008, 322).
- In Mesoamerica, the beginnings of sedentary life marks the start of the Formative, or Preclassic, Period.
- Early centers of the Olmec occur on the Mexican Gulf Coast while El Mirador, an unusually large site for its early date, is found in the Mayan lowlands.
- At the end of the Formative Period, major urban centers develop in the highlands.
- By the onset of the Classic Period (AD 200–300), two of these, Monte Albán and Teotihuacan, grew significantly.
- Teotihuacan became one of the largest cities in the world.
- Other centers with large monumental architecture occur in the Classic Period and are associated with the ancient Maya.
- These include Tikal and Palenque, though numerous other Mayan sites are now known.

- Between AD 700 and 900, Mesoamerican centers and peoples underwent a number of upheavals and changes, leading to the depopulation and collapse of many centers, like Monte Albá, Teotihuacan and Tikal and Palenque slightly later.

- A number of other Mayan sites in the southern areas of Mayan influence were also abandoned or depopulated.
- The exact reasons for the abandonment of these centers remains unclear.
- After this time, at about AD 900, the Postclassic Period begins, during which political integration seems more fragmented and fewer monumental centers were constructed.
- However, a few cities did notably grow during this time, including Tula (the Toltec capital), located on Mesoamerica's northern frontier, and Chichén Itzá, a Mayan site with possible Toltec influences located in the northern part of the Yucatán Peninsula.

- Many of these sites and site complexes can be defined as complex state-level societies (and city-states) and have many of the characteristics listed in Table 14.1.
- Examples of these characteristics can be seen at the sites of Monte Albán and Teotihuacan, interpreted as becoming the centers of state-level complex societies in the Late Preclassic to Classic Periods.

Table 14.1 Some Characteristics of State-Level Complex Societies

1. Centralization of Power
   a. Rank Size of Settlement Hierarchy:
      Cities and surrounding towns/villages
      Corresponds to a four-level settlement hierarchy

2. Communication Network
   a. Road systems
   b. Water routes

3. Monopoly on the use of violence

4. Agrarian/pastoral/marine intensive subsistence base

5. Writing or other forms of accounting systems
   a. Hieroglyphics
   b. Other accounting systems

6. Territorial control based on defined partitioning of internal lands and peoples

7. Specialization of labor and stratification (the creation of separate social strata) leading to class societies
   a. Ruling class
   b. Priestly class
   c. Artesan class or craft specialists
   d. Agricultural /pastoral class

8. Ranking or hierarchical ordering of classes and kinship networks

9. Ideological belief in one creator God with other lesser ranking Gods
   a. Lineage of the ruling elite linked to the Gods
   b. Animistic beliefs of other ethnic groups often left in place

10. Redistribution and tribute
    a. Command political economies
    b. Possible market economies at frontiers

Monte Albán

- Monte Albán is located in the Valley of Oaxaca on a high defensible hilltop away from bottomlands with good farmland.
- By the last centuries BC, it is estimated to have a population of 15,000 greatly surpassing the nearby site of San José Mogote (see Marcus and Flannery 1996, 24; Price and Feinman 2008, 343).
- During the phase known as Monte Albán I (500–200 BC), the first public buildings occur, and more than 500 stone monuments are carved.
- These figures have been called *danzantes* (dancers) but, more likely, represent warriors or a military theme, which becomes evident throughout Mesoamerica after this time period and can be linked to the formation of state-level societies.
- Drawings of slain captives can be found carved on monuments at Monte Albán (Price and Feinman 2008, 341; table from Marcus and Flannery 1996).

- Hilltop location and defensive walls also attest to conflict and the consolidation of power in the valley by Monte Albán II (200 BC–AD 200).
- Concern for the dead and their ancestral ties to the living is found in the construction of elaborate subterranean tombs and the huge North Platform acropolis at the site (Price and Feinman 2008, 339–340).

FIGURE 14.1. The archaeological site of Monte Albán, Valley of Oaxaca, with Building J in the foreground. Photo taken by Hajor; created January 2004.
Copyright © Petrusbarbygere (CC BY-SA 3.0) at http://commons. wikimedia.org/wiki/File:Monte_Alb%C3%A1n_archeological_site,_Oaxaca. jpg.

- Further evidence of conquest comes from Building J, an arrowhead-shaped building with more than 40 carved stone panels. These panels yield early evidence of the use of hieroglyphs and are place names.

- One of these identified locations is Cuicatlán Cañada, 80 kilometers (km) (50 miles) northeast of Monte Albá, where a town was sacked and burned with skulls of 61 of its inhabitants mounted on a skull rack.
- These racks were called *tzompantli* by the Aztec, who utilized them during military campaigns and, apparently, in association with ritual ball games.
- In terms of early hieroglyphic Mesoamerican writings systems, the earliest evidence to date occurs at Monument 3 of San José Mogote in the Late Rosario Phase (sixth century BC) and is indicative of a captive with stylized blood flowing from the chest, identified as "I Earthquake" or "I Eye."
- This name is also indicative of the early use of a 260-day ritual calendric system, whereby individuals obtained their name based on the day and month during which they were born.
- The bas-relief threshold stone from Monument 3 was placed so that anyone entering or leaving the building would have to step on him (Marcus and Flannery 1996, Plate VII).
- During Monte Albán III, a powerful ruler was buried in Tomb 7, from which gold, carved jaguar bones, shell, turquoise, jet, crystal, and other exotic items were recovered.
- Other tombs reveal elaborate grave goods, such as those of a Zapotec lord buried in Tomb 104. Grave offerings indicate a cult of deified ancestors (Coe and Koontz 2002, 128).
- Examples of grave goods: a jade pectoral found with a sacrificial victim (Marcus and Flannery 1996) and a gold pendant from Tomb 7 cast in one piece by the lost-wax method. The elements represent, top to bottom, a ball game played between two gods, the solar disk, a stylized butterfly, and the Earth Monster (Mixtec culture, Late Post-Classic Period. Length 22 cm. Coe and Koontz 2002, 179).

Monte Albán and Characteristics of Complex Societies

- By AD 500–700, numerous characteristics of complex societies occur at the site and in the valley.
- Characteristics include:
- Centralization of power is indicated by a probable four-tier settlement system existing in the valley by Late Monte Albán I.
- Monopoly on the use of violence is indicated by Building J and the *danzante* glyphs.

- An agrarian, intensive subsistence system and large populations is indicated by settlement size and ecofactual remains.
- A writing and a calendric system are indicated by glyphs and the threshold stone at Monument 3 of San José Mogote.
- Territorial control based on partitioning of controlled lands is indicated, again, by glyphs at Building J.
- Specialization of labor with an elite class and craft specialists is indicated by artifacts recovered and burial and monument construction.
- Ranking of kinship groups is indicated by the North Platform acropolis and Tomb 7.
- Tribute and probable redistribution is indicated by the type of artifacts and goods recovered from the site with sources from other areas (see Marcus and Flannery 1996, 190: Five phases of Monte Albán, Valley of Oaxaca, date to 500 BC to AD 1300–1521).

Teotihuacan

- The site has the distinction of being one of the largest cities in the world in AD 500.
- It is located near natural springs in the Valley of Mexico in the Central Highlands at an elevation of 2,100 m (7,000 ft). It is about 20 km from Lake Texcoco.
- By 200 BC, the site had been established, and by AD 100, it was the main settlement in the basin encompassing ca. 20 square km (7.5 square miles) with an estimated population of 90,000.

FIGURE 14.2. The archaeological site of Teotihuacan with the Avenue of the Dead passing in front of the Pyramid of the Sun (to the left). Photo taken from the Pyramid of the Moon. Photo by tirada por mim; created September 2006.
BrCG2007, "Teotihuacan," http://commons.wikimedia.org/wiki/ File:SSA41434.JPG. Copyright in the Public Domain.

- Around AD 700 to 800, the site was partially burned and abandoned (Coe and Koontz 2002: 102; Price and Feinman 2008: 346).

- The manufacture of obsidian goods and trade from south to north in products like ceramics and cacao may have played a role in the city's growth.
- The control of water through the construction of canals from the natural springs may have also led to the site's growth.
- Obsidian mines occur near Teotihuacan (Coe and Koontz 2002; Stuart 1981).
- The site is one of a few in the New World that was initially laid out on a grid pattern.
- Evidence in a belief in gods, such as the sun god and moon goddess, is indicated in the constructions of the monumental architecture of the Pyramid of the Sun and Pyramid of the Moon (these are the names believed to have been given to these monumental constructions by the local inhabitants of the area).
- The grid system also gives evidence of the widespread use of a Mesoamerican numeric system based on a count of 20, which is also the numeric system on which the Mesoamerican ritual calendar is based (Coe and Koontz 2002, 104).

- Sugiyama (2005) indicates that the basic unit of measurement was 83 cm, so that, for instance, the original size of the Sun Pyramid, at 216 square meter (m²) at its base, symbolized the ritual calendar, which has 260 days (83 cm x 260 days = 215.8 m).
- The ancient city has two main axes, the north–south running Avenue of the Dead, which runs from the Pyramid of the Moon past the Pyramid of the Sun to the Ciudadela and the east–west road that runs past the Ciudadela.
- The distances between the axis of the Avenue of the Dead and the eastern limits of both complexes are nearly equal, at 431 m and 432 m, respectively, which is associated to what is called the Calendar Round, a 52-year correspondence between the ritual 260 day calendar and the solar year 365 day calendar (83 cm x 52 years x 10 = 431.6 m) Coe and Koontz 2002, 105).

- The Pyramid of the Sun is the largest monument built in a single construction episode in the ancient Americas.
- The structure is 64 m (212 ft) high and is filled with 1 million m³ of fill carried to the pyramid.
- A cave was discovered under the Pyramid of the Sun, indicating that it was probably an important ritual location even before the pyramid's construction.
- The Pyramid of the Moon was constructed in seven different phases with three sacrificial burial complexes uncovered.

- One of the sacrificial burial complexes in Building 4 is associated with symbols of sacred warfare, including skeletons of sacrificed animals believed to represent military institutions.
- The construction of Building 4 is thought to mark the moment of state development and is dated to the first half of the third century AD.
- The Pyramid of the Moon is 45 m in height and is about 149 m wide by 168 m long.
- No royal tombs have been uncovered from the pyramids (see Price and Feinman 2008, 349).

- The Ciudadela is associated with military activities and the Temple of the Feathered Serpent.
- Within the Ciudadela is the last public monument built at Teotihuacan (early in the third century AD), the Temple of Quetzalcoatl, in which more than 200 sacrificial victims were identified. Most of these were young warriors with their hands tied behind their backs in two groups of 18 (the number of months in the solar year calendar).
- Many of these wear necklaces of human jaws, upper and lower, some real and some made of shell.
- Quetzalcoatl is identified as the Aztec hero-god, god of life, and creator of humanity from his own blood.
- The west façade of the Temple of Quetzalcoatl, Teotihuacan, marks the transition between the Late Preclassic and Classic Periods. Feathered serpents flank the stairway, and serpent heads undulate on the slopping batters with fire serpent heads alternating with feathered serpents within the entablatures. Note the duality between the sky serpent motif and the earth fire monster (jaguar) motif (Coe and Koontz 2002, 109–110).

Teotihuacan and Characteristics of Complex Societies

- By AD 100 to 500, numerous characteristics of complex societies occurred at the site.
- Characteristics include:
- Centralization of power is indicated by the predetermined site plan and size of Teotihuacan.

- Monopoly on the use of violence is indicated by Building 4 of the Temple of the Moon, which is associated with symbols of sacred warfare, and by the Temple of Quetzalcoatl, in which more than 200 sacrificial victims were identified.
- An agrarian, intensive subsistence system and large populations are indicated by settlement size and ecofactual remains.
- A writing/numeric and calendric system are indicated by the layout of the site and dimensions of major architectural monuments.
- Territorial control may be seen in the evidence of sacrificial victims.
- Specialization of labor with an elite class and craft specialists is indicated by artifacts recovered and monumental constructions.
- Ranking of kinship groups is indicated by the location of elite residences close to the main avenues of the site.
- Tribute and probable redistribution is indicated by the type of artifacts and goods recovered from the site with sources from other areas and the recovery of obsidian from other locations in Mesoamerica with origins that are close to Teotihuacan.

PART FOUR

Linguistics

CHAPTER FIFTEEN

Language and Linguistics

Introduction

- What does the study of linguistics entail?
- Language is the cognitive boundary between primates and humans.
- Great apes have communication systems but no syntax.
- Syntax: the arrangements of words into sentences (i.e., Jane goes to the store.).
- Language production and comprehension is related to the development of certain areas in the human brain.
- Language is produced in the Broca's area of the brain.
- The Wernicke area of the brain controls language comprehension.
- Other physical differences between primates and humans related to language include the position of the larynx and epiglottis and the size of tongue.
- Larynx: sound-making organ in the throat.
- Epiglottis: flat cartilage over the glottis (the opening between the vocal cords in the larynx).
- Human larynx placed much lower in throat to enhance our ability to speak.
- Human tongue is shorter and thicker to allow for a wider range of vowel sounds.

- For more in-depth coverage of the material found in this chapter and the next, see Finegan (2015).

Descriptive Linguistics

Main Concepts

- Phonics: producing sound.
- Phonetics: the science that deals with pronunciation and the representation of sounds in speech.
- Phonology: the study of sound patterns of human language (i.e., speech utterances as sequences of sound, f in food, gh in tough, ph in phone).
- Phonemes: the minimal unit of language. A sound or set of sounds that makes a difference in meaning in that language. Example: fine, vine, chunk, junk.
- Morphology: the study of the words that make up language.
- Morpheme: the minimal unit of meaning or minimal linguistic sign. Example: one morpheme - desire; two morphemes - desire+able.
- Syntax: the arrangement of words in a sentence.
- Surface structure: the lineal order that is observed in morphemes and words.
- Deep structure: abstract level of syntax structure.

A Few Major Scholars' Areas of Interest in the Field of Linguistics

- Noam Chomsky (1928–Present) (1981, 1965, 1957). Father of transformational linguistics. All languages have a common structural basis (i.e., people can learn different languages).
- See differing points of view on this by linguist Daniel Everett (2008) and his research with the Piraha of Southwestern Brazil (for instance the YouTube video "Out on a Limb Over Language") disputing if all humans have a common structural basis to their languages. For example, recursion, which is the ability to place one phrase inside another, is discussed in the video.

- Kenneth Pike (1912–2010). Linguistic concepts of etic and emic.
- Emic: categories devised by the native point of view, nonstructural results.
- Etic: categories devised by the researcher's point of view, structural results. Field of ethnoscience.

- Edward Sapir (1884–1939) and Benjamin Whorf (1897–1941). The Sapir-Whorf hypothesis posits that language limits or determines culture and shapes the way you think and behave (Finegan 2015; Sapir 1921).
- Example: the conceptualization of time in different ways. The Hopi of the Southwest U.S. have no way of saying a specific stretch of time. They do not conceptualize time in the sense of units that can be measured. On the other hand, English speakers can say "my fifteen minutes of fame" and conceive of time as a finite source or entity that can be measured.

Historical or Comparative Linguistics

- Historical, or comparative, linguistics study how languages change over time.
- Proto-language: a reconstructed language.
- Language family: languages that derive from the same proto-language.
- Language families exist over large areas, because they have spread in different ways from homeland areas.
- How might this have happened? The spread of language families appears to be linked to the spread of archaeological complexes originating in areas where agriculture or food production was first initiated.
- Archaeological and biological evidence now indicates that the spread of certain archaeological complexes and languages appears to be due to the increase in population and migration from areas where agriculture originated.
- For more information on this subject, see Bellwood (2013, 2005).

Diversity of Languages

- The areas with the highest diversity of languages seem to correlate with the environments with the richest diversity of plants and animals.
- One belt is West and Central Africa; another is South and Southeast Asia and the Pacific.

Languages Today: 7,102 (2015)		
Africa	2,138	30%
Pacific	1,313	18.50%
Americas	1,064	15%
Asia	2,301	32%
Europe	286	4%

Table 15.1. Anderson, "Languages Today," From www.ethnologue.com AND Anderson, Stephen R. 2010. How Many Languages Are There in the World? Brochure Series: Frequently Asked Questions. Linguistic Society of America, Washington, DC.

- The country with the most diversity is Papua New Guinea, with 862 languages. Papua New Guinea only has 0.4% of the world's land area.
- Language transmission seems to be rooted in an economic system of social bonds.
- Social bonds help people to manage ecological risk.
- The greater the ecological risk in some areas of the world, the broader the social network and the less diverse the numbers of languages.
- Today, most of the languages of the world are believed to be in the process of extinction. Likely, 85% of the languages of the world may disappear in less than 20 years.

CHAPTER SIXTEEN

Historical Linguistics, Early Migrations, and Language Diversity

Historical or Comparative Linguistics

- As indicated in the previous chapter, languages change over time.

Migration in Prehistoric Times

- Migration has been, and is, a basic aspect of human adaptation.
- There are three well-researched phases of human migration in prehistory and a fourth in historic times.
- The following list and information in this section are derived from Bellwood (2013) unless noted otherwise.
    1. Migrations of the extinct members of the genus *Homo*, such as *Homo erectus* and Neanderthals, after about 2.5 million years ago, within and out of Africa.
    2. Migrations of ancestral modern humans (*Homo sapiens*) throughout most of the world, including Australia and the Americas, between about 120,000 and 25,000 years ago.
    3. Migrations of herders, farmers, and boat builders in a number of separate waves in various parts of the world, except Antarctica, during the last 10,000 years.

- The third migration of herders, farmers, and boat builders during the last 10,000 years is of interest when examining why we speak the languages that we do.

- How Do We Know That These Migrations Occurred?
    1. Linguistic Evidence.
    2. Archaeological Evidence.
    3. Genetic/Biological Evidence.

- Maps of the Old World major language family distributions at ca. AD 1500 and those of the centers of origin for agriculture in the Old World reveal close correlations between the movement of peoples, languages, and archaeological complexes.

Four Major Regions of Food Production and Migrations

1. The Fertile Crescent of Western Asia

- Origins of wheat, barley, sheep, goats, pigs, cattle, peas, broad beans, and lentils.
- System spread with human migrations between ca. 8500 and 3000 BC.
- Migrations included to the Middle East, Northwestern India, the Mediterranean, temperate Europe, Central Asian steppes and semi-deserts, and North Africa.
- Western Asia (Middle East) and Europe: archaeological evidence, linguistic evidence, genetic/biological evidence.

- Did the origins of agriculture and the Neolithic Revolution spread from the Middle East to Europe through an exchange of technology or through a migration of peoples (gene flow)?
- Using principal components analysis and the gene frequencies of certain traits for populations in these regions, Cavalli-Sforza and Cavalli-Sforza (1996) were able to show a gradient in genetic composition that spread from the Middle East to Europe.
- This gradient in gene frequencies can be interpreted as evidence of an actual migration of peoples with their technology. The study looked at the genetic landscape of Europe using the first principal component of the frequencies of 95 genes (Cavalli-Sforza and Cavalli-Sforza 1996).
- Example: the Rh factor. This is a substance found in the blood of some humans, named after the *Macacus rhesus* monkey, which also contains the substance.

- Rh+ is more common in the Middle East; Rh- is prevalent in Western Europe.
- Genetic gradation of gene frequencies for this factor reveal that people with Rh+ blood types migrated from the Middle East to mix with people originally of Rh- blood types (Cavalli-Sforza and Cavalli-Sforza 1996).

2. The Yellow and Yangzi Basins of China

- Origins of short grain rice, foxtail and common millet, soybeans, pigs, chicken, indigenous cattle, and the silkworm.
- System spread with human migrations between ca. 4000 and 1000 BC.
- Migrations spread to Northern India, Western China, Tibet, and most of Southeast Asia.
- East and Southeast Asia (China): linguistic evidence

3. Northern Sub-Saharan Africa

- Origins of some yam species, West African species of rice and several species of millet (i.e., pearl millet, finger millet, and sorghum).
- System spread between ca. 5000 and 3000 years ago.
- Migrations spread through monsoonal regions of Sub-Saharan Africa.
- Africa: linguistic evidence

4. Mesoamerica

- Origins of maize, some species of beans and squash, tomatoes, and possibly, some species of chile pepper, avocado, and turkey.
- Systems spread with human migrations after ca. 2000 BC.
- Migrations spread into the U.S. Southwest and the Andes (later into Eastern U.S. without evidence of migrations).
- New World major language family distributions at ca. AD 1500 can also be compared to the centers of the origins of agriculture in the New World.

Four other regions of the origins of food production with less migratory influence

1. Western Pacific
2. South Asia
3. The Central Andes
4. The Eastern Woodlands of the United States

PART FIVE

Cultural Anthropology

CHAPTER SEVENTEEN

Culture: The Origins of the Concept

From Civilization to Culture: Civilization

- Before there were cultures, the concept of civilization was used.
- Civilization, as a technical legal term, refers to the conversion of a criminal prosecution into a civil matter.
- This concept also changed through time until it became an ideological concept attached to the idea of lineal progress, where the dominant societies were the examples of civilization.
- The concept started to collapse with the two world wars and gradually became replaced with the concept of culture.

From Civilization to Culture: Culture

- The word is derived from the past participle of the Latin verb *colere*, "to cultivate."
- In Middle English, *cultura* meant "a plowed field;" in German, it is *Kultur* in the sense of cultivation.
- Later the word was used in relation to progressive refinement and breeding in domestication of some particular crop. Examples: culture of the vine or a bacterial culture.
- Today, we have different meanings for the concept.

The Historical Change of the Concept: What is Culture in Anthropology?

- Since the end of the nineteenth century, the concept of Culture seems to be related to knowledge and beliefs that are learned (example in Edward Tylor's work [1871]).
- Later in the beginning of the twentieth century, the concept changed to that related to habits or behavior that is learned and reproduced by the group (example in Franz Boas' work [1938]).
- After the world wars, it began to be seen as a set of unconscious rules that integrate individuals.

The Concept as Diverse as the Theoretical Orientation of the Anthropologist: Two Cases

Alfred Louis Kroeber (1876-1960)

- Professor at University of California, Berkeley.
- History determined by cultural patterns not the individual.
- Super-organic forces shape the individual.
- Impossible to do cross cultural comparison.

Margaret Mead (1901–1978)

- Culture, not biology or race, determines variation in human behavior. In other words, culture is learned in the process of construction of an individual personality.

Ruth Benedict (1887–1947)

- Culture was a projection of the personality of those who created it.
- She looked for cultural patterns that were based on generalist types, such as "Dyonysian, Apollinian, and Paranoid" (Benedict 1934).

Where is Culture?

- Culture is in the heads of people.
- Culture is in the materials or artifacts that humans make.
- Culture is in the language.
- Culture is cognitive behavior

Edward Sapir (1884–1939)

- Culture is often spoken of as a code or program.
- Culture is limited by language.

Today's Concept of Culture

- Culture is learned, adaptable, symbolic behavior.
- Culture is a set of learned behaviors and ideas that humans acquire as members of society.
- Humans use culture to adapt and transform the world in which we live.

Cultural Relativism

- The basic premise: our beliefs, morals, behaviors, and perceptions of the world are learned. As a consequence, they are the product of culture.
- Ethnocentrism is the tendency to view one's own culture as superior and to apply one's own cultural values in judging the behavior and beliefs of people raised in other cultures.
- However, because we cannot be objective, we cannot argue that there is one culture above others.
- In this sense, cultures can only be judged relative to one another. Any interpretation has to be given in the context of a particular culture and history.

Cultural Historical Particularism

- Also the singular history of each culture makes the generalization of a universal history impossible.
- We can only make particular histories of cultures.

- In many texts today, culture is also seen as accumulated building blocks of knowledge that are transmitted through learning.

Cultural Comparison

George Peter Murdock (1897–1985)

- Comparison of cultures as systems.
- The Human Relations Area Files: can now be easily accessed at www.hraf.yale.edu.
- Their mission statement reads: "Founded in 1949 at Yale University, the Human Relations Area Files, Inc., (HRAF) is an internationally recognized organization in the field of cultural anthropology. HRAF's mission is to encourage and facilitate the cross-cultural study of human culture, society, and behavior in the past and present. HRAF produces two online databases: eHRAF World Cultures and eHRAF Archaeology, and other resources for teaching and research" (as cited on their website at www.hraf.yale.edu).

Further Cultural Approaches to Anthropology

- Some of the major schools of thought in anthropology include those described below.
- For a more extensive list of these approaches, return to Chapter 2 for a brief description and a list of the major scholars and their publications for each.
- Schools of Thought:
- The cultural-personality school
- The cultural evolutionary school
- The cultural ecology school
- Cultural materialism
- Cultural critique or postmodern culturalism

The Cultural-personality School

- Freudian and non-Freudian approaches: determinants of personality.
- Margaret Mead (1901–1978). Reflection on teenage sexuality in U.S. Publications: *Coming of Age in Samoa* (1949 [1928]) and *Sex and Temperament in Three Primitive Societies* (1935).

- Ruth Fulton Benedict (1887–1948). The behavior of the individual in a culture. Publication: *The Chrysanthemum and the Sword* (1946).
- Ralph Linton (1893–1953). Concepts of status and role, cultural personality, influenced by Max Weber, ascribed and achieved status. Publications: *The Study of Man* (1936) and *The Tree of Culture* (1955).
- Oscar Lewis' (1914–1970). The culture of poverty. Poverty breeds a particular variety of personality. Publications: *Five Families: Mexican Case Studies in the Culture of Poverty* (1959) and *La Vida: A Puerto Rican Family in the Culture of Poverty—San Juan and New York* (1966).

Cultural Evolutionary School

- Leslie A. White (1900–1975). Professor at the University of Michigan, Ann Arbor. Publication*: The Evolution of Culture* (1959).
- A culture is a thermodynamic system. Culture is an organization of things in motion, a process of energy transformation.

- Culture evolves. One form grows into another.
- An evolutionary stage is one succession of forms in the developmental process.
- The best way to measure cultures is by the amount of energy harnessed per capita per year.
- We can evaluate cultures and arrange them in a series from lower to higher.

The Cultural Ecology School

- Julian Steward (1902–1972). Student of Alfred Kroeber. Professor at the University of Illinois at Urbana. Cultural ecology is the study of the processes by which a society adapts to its environment. Editor of the Smithsonian Institution's *Handbook of South American Indians* (1963). Publication: *Theory of Culture Change: The Methodology of Multilinear Evolution* (1955).
- Adaptation: a natural process by which humans develop strategies to cope with the environment. Focus on subsistence and economic arrangements.
- The case of Roy Rappaport (1926–1997) and the pigs of New Guinea. Publication: *Pigs for the ancestors: Ritual in the ecology of a New Guinea people* (1967).

Cultural Materialism

- Marvin Harris (1927–2001). Professor at Columbia and, later, the University of Florida at Gainesville. Publication: *Cows, Pigs, Wars, & Witches: The Riddles of Culture* (1989) and *Cultural Materialism: The Struggle for a Science of Culture* (1979).
- Offered a mechanistic explanation of culture as comprised of a core infrastructure (technology, economy, and demography) that determines the structure (social relations, kinship and descent, and patterns of distribution and consumption) and superstructure (religion, ideology, and play) of the culture. Critiques include that hypotheses developed using this approach are difficult, if not impossible, to evaluate scientifically.

Cultural Critique or Postmodernist–Cultural School

- Clifford Geertz (1926–2006). The interpretation of cultures. Bali and Java fieldwork. Publication: *Peddlers and Princes: Social Change and Economic Modernization in Two Indonesian Towns* (1963).
- Culture is a stylistic expression or symbolic actions. Cultures can be "read" in different forms. As a consequence, there is variation in the "text" that we can produce from them.
- To study the other leads toward reflection on ourselves.

Conclusions

- The concept of culture has evolved through time. Today, culture is accepted as learned behaviors that integrate individuals that share similar processes of learning.

- Cultural anthropology is a diverse field that has developed according to historical questions about ourselves, such as:
- How our personality developed and what is learned from institutions and human relations
- How our institutions evolved
- How we and the other interact with the environment
- How our material lives shape our beliefs
- How we see the other and what it means in relation to ourselves

CHAPTER EIGHTEEN

Systems of Food Collection and Production

- The uses of plants and animals by humans and how this relationship affects human behaviors and strategies for survival.

The Difference Between Wild, Semi-Domesticated, and Domesticated Plants

- The food production and domestication process of plants and animals is a continuum that runs from foraging of wild plants and cultivation of semi-domesticated plants to full domestication and agriculture.
- This continuum involves varying behaviors, including foraging, plant husbandry, horticulture, and agriculture.
- One must understand the difference between agriculture (a human technological innovation and change in human behavior) versus domestication (a genetic change evident in plant structures).
- See further information in Ford (1985).

- Domestication: the genetic changes to plants and animals that are caused by unintentional or intentional human manipulation and result in the dependence of the plant or animal on humans for its reproduction.

Types of Human Subsistence Systems Used to Obtain Plant Resources

- Foraging and Collecting: the search for and collection of useful plant parts without intentional planting or changes to the landscape

- Managing: the maintenance of important plants without intentional planting.
- Cultivation/Horticulture: the intentional planting, tending, and harvesting of plants with changes to the landscape.
- Agriculture: large-scale, labor-intensive production of plants. Changes to the landscape are obvious. The two types are extensive and intensive agriculture.

Some Theories on the Development of Food Production

Optimal Foraging Theory

- Optimal Foraging Theory: generally, species with higher energy yields (high-ranked) will be chosen first for food, while species with a lower energy yield (low-ranked) will be ignored or will only be chosen if higher-ranked resources are not available.

Broad Spectrum Revolution

- Broad Spectrum Revolution: the transition to farming involved a period in which foragers broadened their resource base to encompass a wide variety of foods that were previously ignored in an attempt to overcome food shortages (Flannery 1986, 1973; also, see Pianka 1988, 173).
- Example: Ohalo II (23000 BP), Israel, where the majority of plant remains found were of wild grasses, including wild cereals of wheat and barley (Nadel et al. 2012).

Risk Management Theories

- Risk Management Theories: Theories developed to describe human strategies to reduce risk.
- Risk: the probability of a loss, hazard, or falling below some fixed level of consumption, or the unpredictable variation in an economic or ecological variable (Cashdan 1990, 2–3; Hames 1990; Hames and Vickers 1983).
- In general, risk management studies have noted three ways to reduce risk. These include food storage, changes in the diet breadth, and food sharing or pooling. The first two solutions can be accomplished within the nuclear family. The third

requires interaction/cooperation with other group(s) of foragers (Hames 1990; Hames and Vickers 1983).

- Agricultural Intensification: "the process of increasing labor, knowledge, and technological efficiency to produce increased food energy and/or to increase security by minimizing risks" (Gallagher and Arzigian 1994, 171).

Types of Human Subsistence Systems Used to Obtain Plant Resources

Foraging and Collecting

- Foraging and Collecting: the search for and collection of useful plant parts without intentional planting.
- This subsistence strategy also includes hunting and fishing of wild animals.
- Example: The Nukak, Colombian Amazon (Cabrera et al. 1999).
- Residential mobility. Movement of group to resources. For instance the Nukak have been recorded to have ca. 69 camps per year with each occupied about 5.3 days.
- Logistic mobility. Use of base camps. Movement of task groups to resources (Cabrera et al. 1999).
- Large territories.
- Seasonal movements based on resource availability (Cabrera et al. 1999).

Managing (Plant Husbandry)

- Managing (Plant Husbandry): the maintenance of important plants without intentional planting (Cabrera et al. 1999).

Cultivation and Horticulture

- Cultivation and Horticulture: the intentional planting, tending, and harvesting of plants.
- Landscape modification.
- Continuum from mobile to semi-sedentary to sedentary (staying in one place for most of the year).

Extensive Agricultural Systems

- Extensive Agricultural Systems
- Examples: Slash and burn agriculture, arboreal culture
- Semi-sedentary to sedentary (Chagnon 1983)
- Maintenance of a diversity of crops within a field
- Use of fallow to replenish soils
- Seasonal cycle of cutting, burning, planting, and harvest (Cabrera et al. 1999)

Intensive Agricultural Systems

- Intensive Agricultural Systems
- Examples: monocropping. Industrial agriculture.
- Sedentary societies
- Focus on one or few crops within a field (for instance present-day rice cultivation near Wang-Dong Cave in Jiangxi Province, China) (Smith 1998)
- Example: quinoa (*Chenopodium quinoa*) grown in high-altitude basins and valleys of the Andes, South America (Smith 1998).
- Large- scale landscape modification. Use of terraces, irrigation, and fertilizers to replenish soils.
- Narrow rice terraces near Guilin, China (Smith 1998)

Huitoto chagra: tierra firme

FIGURE 18.1. Slash and burn field or chagra in tierra firme of the Huitoto indigenous group outside of Leticia, Department of Amazonas, Colombia, 1997–1998. Photo by Renée M. Bonzani.

FIGURE 18.2. Manioc (*Manihot esculenta*) growing on the floodplain of the Amazon River near Leticia, Department of Amazonas, Colombia, 1997–1998. Photo by Renée M. Bonzani.

Animal Husbandry

- The following definitions are from Clutton-Brock (1989).

- Hunters: food-extractors who are only interested in dead animals. They interact with prey when it is about to be killed.
- Herd-followers: may correspond to a human population that ranges over the same area in its annual cycle as the animal population or apply to particular humans that are associated with particular herds of animals, which is equivalent to ranching.
- Examples include the Sámi (Lapps) reindeer-herders in Norway, Sweden, Finland, and Russia (Aikio 1989).
- The rancher loosely owns herds of animals for exploitation of meat and other resources that are often marketed. The animals may be wild, feral, or domestic, but they live as wild animals except that their territory is usually restricted.
- Nomads may be wandering hunter-gatherers or mobile pastoralists.
- Pastoralists live in North Africa, the Middle East, Europe, Asia, and sub-Saharan Africa.
- They are herders whose activities focus on such domesticated animals as cattle, sheep, goats, camels, and yak.
- Pastoralists are divided into two broad groups.
- Pastoral nomadism proper: characterized by an absence of agriculture as in the Sahara Desert. The entire group—men, women and children—move with the animals throughout the year. These groups are frequently found in the Middle East and North Africa. They trade for crops.
- Semi-nomadic pastoralism: when part of the group moves the herd periodically to new pastures but most people stay in the home village. The most common type of animal husbandry group. These groups produce their own crops in the home village. Examples: Europe and Africa.
- Transhumants are agriculturalists who move their livestock between mountain and lowland pastures. They are found in the Mediterranean and Southern Europe, also in the Andes Mountains of South America.
- Examples include llama herders in the farthest part of Northwest Argentina. In this area, two herding systems are based on seasonality. For instance, hill people live at base camps in the rainy season from November to the beginning of April. Then, the llamas move up the mountains in the dry season from April to October.

Herders follow the llamas and stay there until the next change of seasons (Rabey 1986).

- One can compare maps on world ecological regions to different aspects of culture like kinship patterns and world religions to look for possible correlations (Allen and Shalinsky 2004).

Summary on Pastoralism

- Occurs in semi-arid to arid conditions
- Involves a nomadic lifestyle based on the herding of livestock
- Polygyny, or multiple marriages and large families, are common
- Kinship structures based on the clan and can be extensive in territorial control
- Work routines, ethics, and structure are different from agricultural societies
- As industrializing horticultural/pastoral societies, population growth rates are high. Thus, growth in productivity is eliminated by the population growth rate, causing poverty and a reduction in the standard of living.
- World religion tends to be Islamic

Origins of Social and Political Diversification: The Family Level

Introduction

- Humans are social animals. As a consequence, they create institutions that also reproduce in time and space.
- Social institutions vary according to the demographic scale of the group or communities.
- Social institutions also create "identity." This individual identity varies from the self to the family to the political institutions to which the individual identifies as belonging.
- Identity is based on the individual's perception of space and time or her/his conception of territoriality. This can change through time.
- Remember that natural selection works at the level of the individual. It is the individual who makes choices as to what groups she/he belongs in order to increase her/his reproductive success.
- The origins of social evolutions are based on the family structure, or the basic family unit.
- Since the beginning of food production, the continued population growth demands more complex structures of organization that increase in scale and complexity in relation to the control of resources and the reproduction of the groups.

1. Family level
   - We have as social institutions: kinship systems, marriage patterns, descent groups.
2. Community level
   - Mechanisms for promoting egalitarianism, hierarchies, positions, or rights; ascribed and achieved.
3. Inter-community level
   - The diversity of arrangements is based on grades from kinship to political and economic affiliations.
   - These forms are bands, tribes, chiefdoms, states, and nation-states.

1. Family Level: The Kinship Basis of Social Evolution

- Kinship: The allocation of rights and their transmission from one generation to the next. These rights are as diverse as, for example, group membership, succession to office, inheritance of property, locality of residence, types of occupation, and other cultural aspects.

Basic Concepts of Kinship

- Minimal nuclear unit: the mother and the offspring.
- Nuclear family: A unit consisting typically of a married man and woman with their offspring.

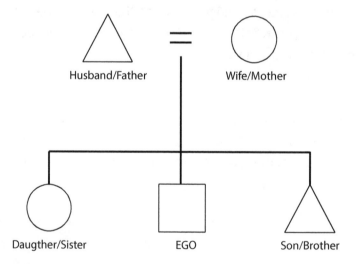

FIGURE 19.1. Diagram of the nuclear family: A unit consisting typically of a married man and woman with their offspring.

- Extended family: a unit composed of two or more nuclear families linked by consanguineal ties.
- Family by choice: male and male arrangements or female and female arrangements to form a family unit.
- Consanguinity: "same blood."
- Affinity: relationship resulting from marriage rather than from descent from a common ancestor.
- Cross Cousins: the children of a father's sister or of a mother's brother; the children of siblings of the opposite sex.
- Parallel Cousins: the children of siblings of the same sex. The children of a father's brother and a mother's sister.

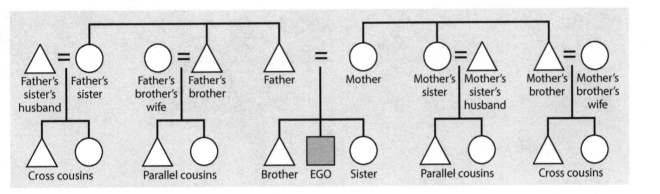

FIGURE 19.2. Diagram of the relationship between cross cousins and parallel cousins.

- Lineal relatives: relatives from the ascending or descending generation from the father's or mother's lines, as well as offspring.
- Lateral relatives: kin on the side of the brother and sister of the mother or the father.

Inheritance Rules

- Primogeniture: inheritance through the first born son.
- Patrilineal inheritance: inheritance through the line of the father.
- Matrilineal inheritance: inheritance through the line of the mother.

Principles of Descent

- Unilineal descent: traces relationship through either the male or the female line.
- Patrilineal descent: traces descent through the father's side.

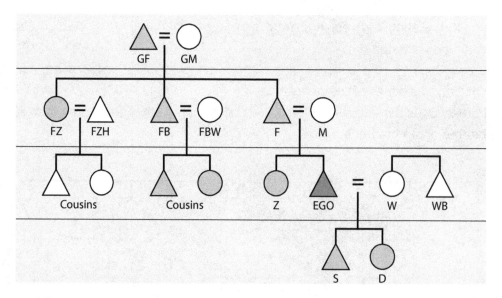

FIGURE 19.3. Diagram of patrilineal descent groups.

- Matrilineal descent: traces descent through the mother's side. Mother's brother is the main male authority.

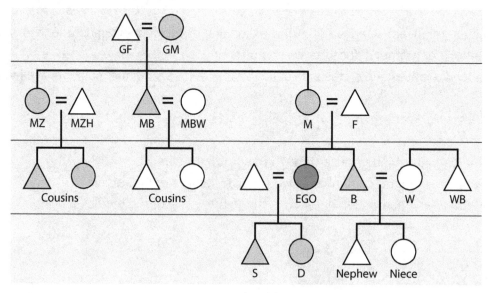

FIGURE 19.4. Diagram of matrilineal descent groups.

- Bilineal descent: a practice that links a person with a group of matrilineal and patrilineal ties.

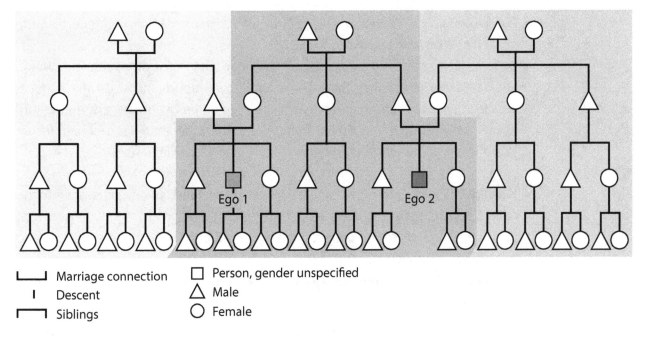

```
⌐__⌐  Marriage connection      ☐  Person, gender unspecified
  ǀ    Descent                 △  Male
⌐‾‾⌐  Siblings                 ◯  Female
```

FIGURE 19.5. Diagram of bilineal descent: a practice which links a person with a group of matrilineal and patrilineal ties.

- Ambilineal, or cognatic, descent: each individual has the option of affiliating with either the mother's or father's descent group.

Marriage

- Monogamy: the marriage of one person to one other person.
- Polygamy: multiple marriages.
- Polygyny: the marriage of one man to two or more women at the same time.
- Polyandry: the marriage of one woman to two or more men at the same time.
- Serial monogamy: multiple marriages through time.
- For more in-depth information on these concepts, see Fox (1967).

Marriage: Theory of Alliance or Principles of Reciprocity

- Claude Lévi-Strauss (1908–2009).Concept of structuralism.
- Publications: *The Elementary Structures of Kinship* (1969), *The Raw and the Cooked* (1969), *The Savage Mind* (1966).
- Culture is a surface representation of underlying mental structures. These structures are affected by the physical and social environment. On the surface, people's belief systems can appear to be very different. However, the structure of their belief systems is similar from one group to another. For example, incest taboo is the cornerstone of the structures found in marriage rules.

- Kinship: The allocation of rights and their transmission from one generation to the next. These rights are as diverse as, for example, group membership, succession to office, inheritance of property, locality of residence, types of occupation, and other cultural aspects.
- The study of kinship examines of how people classify others around them and how they classify kin relations.

Marriage as Exchange

- Generalized exchange: relationships between any number of partners.
- Restricted exchange: a mechanism of reciprocity that operates only between two partners or between partners in multiples of two. Example: cross cousin marriage and moieties.

- Dowry: The property endowment, which a bride brings with her into her husband's domestic household at the time of marriage.
- Bridewealth or brideprice: payments from the husband and his kin to the kin of the bride.
- Bride service: payment in work, for a time, to the kin of the bride.

- Levirate: a man marries his brother's widow.
- Sororate: a woman marries her sister's widower.

- Preferred marriage
- Prescribed marriage

Marriage Residence

- Rules of exogamy: marriage rules that require a person to marry outside locale, kin, status, or other such groups to which the person belongs. Example: village exogamy, moieties.
- Rules of endogamy: marriage rules that require a person to marry inside the locale, kin, status, or other such groups to which the person belongs. Example: caste endogamy.
- Patrilocal or virilocal: a norm that requires the bride to reside with the groom either nearby to, or in the home of, the groom's parents.
- Matrilocal or uxorilocal: a norm that requires the groom to leave his paternal home to live with his bride, either nearby to, or in the house of, her parents.
- Avunculocal residence: a norm in which unmarried males leave their parent's home to reside with their mother's brother; upon marriage, their wives are brought into this household.
- Ambilocal residence: married partners may live with either the husband's or wife's group.
- Neolocal: the establishment of an independent household.

Classificatory Terminology

- See Kottak (2013, 440–443).

Primary Kin Types

Father	Fa	F	F
Mother	Mo	M	M
Husband	Hu	H	H
Wife	Wi	W	W
Brother	Br	B	B
Sister	Si	Z	S
Son	So	S	s
Daughter	Da	D	d

△	Signifies male
○	Signifies female
☐	Signifies an individual of either sex
▬	Signifies is married to
≠	Signifies is divorced from
|	Signifies is decended from

	Signifies is a sibling of
▲	Signifies male whose kin are shown
●	Signfies female whose kin are shown
■	Signifies an individual (ego) whose kin are shown
◬	Signifies is deceased
⊘	Signifies is deceased
◉	Signifies an adopted female
≈	Signifies cohabitation
▬	Signifies sexual relation

Table 19.1. Kottak, Fox, Driver, Walter, "Primary Kin Types," http://www. uwgb.edu/walterl/kinship/304Symbols.htm. Copyright in the Public Domain.

- Four systems of kinship terminology include:
  1. Lineal kinship terminology associated to the nuclear family with neolocal residence patterns and often found in industrial or foraging societies.
  2. Bifurcate merging kinship terminology associated to unilineal descent groups, either patrilineal or matrilineal, with patrilocal or matrilocal residence patterns and often found in horticultural, pastoral, and agricultural societies.
  3. Generational kinship terminology associated with ambilineal descent groups and the band with ambilocal residence patterns and often found in agricultural, horticultural, and foraging societies.
  4. Bifurcate collateral kinship terminology associated to various kin and descent groups with various residence patterns and economies.

CHAPTER TWENTY

Origins of Social and Political Diversification: The Supra-Family Levels

Community Level of Societies: From Egalitarian Societies to Stratified Societies

Egalitarian Societies

- The two basic units of social organization among foragers are the nuclear family and the band.
- Typically, the band exists only seasonally, breaking up into nuclear families when subsistence means require it.
- Foraging bands have little ascribed power and authority differentiation. The functions given to law in more complex societies are embedded in the broader matrix of social mores and prescribed behaviors.

Ranked Societies

- Ranked societies are societies comprised of kinship groups that vary in prestige or social esteem. Prestige can be defined as esteem based on social relations, notably by people in neighboring communities and kinship structures, and it is not a physical resource (Clark and Blake 1994).
- Lineage: a consanguineal kin group practicing unilineal descent, which includes persons who can trace their relationship to a common ancestor; that is, a lineage is all the unilineal descendants of a known common ancestor or ancestors.

- Clans: a compromise kin group based on a rule of residence and a rule of descent. The clan is a group composed of a number of lineages.
- A clan is a descent group that claims common descent from an apical ancestor but cannot demonstrate it (stipulated descent). When a clan's apical ancestor is non-human, it is called a totem.
- Examples would include the seven clans of the Cherokee (Wild Potato Clan, Long Hair Clan, Deer Clan, Bird Clan, Blue Holly Clan, Paint Clan, and Wolf Clan).
- Moieties: when a society is divided in two groups so that every person is necessarily a member of one or the other.

Forms of Rank

- Ascribed positions: the right to a position is defined at birth based on the kinship of an individual.
- Achieved rank: positions obtained by age, consensus, or merit.
- Age sets: a group of individuals that share the characteristic of being born in the same time span, such as five years. Their position in the village is defined by age. Example: bachelors of the Kayapo. Usually they participate in rituals that are shared by the same age group.
- Age grades: the sequence of status of those age sets. Example: junior, senior, elders. In several societies, the juniors are the warriors of a group.

Stratified Societies

- The creation of separate social strata is called stratification. Its emergence indicates the transition from chiefdom to state (Kottak 2013, 390-391).
- A stratum is one of two or more groups that are contrasted in social status and access to resources.
- Each stratum has people of all ages and both sexes.

- Max Weber (1864–1920) (1968 [1922]) identified three dimensions to social stratification:
  1. Economic status or wealth, including a person's material assets
  2. Power or the ability to exercise one's will over others or to get others to do things

3. Prestige or the basis of social status refers to esteem, respect, and approval for acts, deeds, or qualities thought of as exemplary

- Castes: societies to which membership and types of labor are ascribed at birth and in which social mobility between groups or sets is not allowed.
- Class: defined not by kinship but by the degree of access to valued resources in a society, namely, wealth, power, and prestige. It is usually defined in economic terms. Marx recognizes two divisions in class societies—the Bourgeoisie, which owns the means of production (tools, knowledge, and raw materials), and the proletariat, or working class, which own their labor power.

Inter-Community Level: Variation in Political Organization

Types of Power Positions

- Leadership: characterized by the capacity to mobilize other individuals into action; an achieved form of power.
- Great Men or Big Men: characterized as individuals that, because of their achievements in warfare or hunting, maintain the political office of a group. Examples: the Baruya and the Etoro of Papua New Guinea.
- Chiefs: an ascribed position by inheritance whereby the chieftainship is obtained through the person's relationship to and position within the dominant kin group of a political unit.

Bands

- The oldest form of political organization, characterized by being of small scale (up to 50 individuals), that depend on gathering and hunting. Power is achieved. Example: the !Kung San (South Africa), the Maku (Brazil, Colombia, and Venezuela), and Mbuti (Zaire).

Tribes

- Horticultural/pastoral groups where there is competition for power between kin groups; they are small in demographic scale; and power is limited to the settlement. For example: the Yanomamö (Venezuela), the indigenous groups of highland Papua New Guinea.

Chiefdoms or Rank Societies

- Ascribed positions based on the lineage or rank of individuals controlling an area through alliances by marriage and warfare. The chiefs monopolize the use of force and are able to organize a system of tax collectors, as well. Sometimes, those individuals are captured in war, and are incorporated as slaves.

States or Nation-States

- The state is/are the agency or agencies within a society that have "the monopoly on the legitimate use of physical force within a given territory" or the monopoly on violence. This definition by Max Weber (2015) was first published in 1919 from his lecture notes in German in "The Profession and Vocation of Politics" (*"Politik als Beruf"*)(2013 [1919]). This definition implies a centralization of power and is a key component of state level societies. Other characteristics of the state include a large population and subsystems with specialized functions including population control, the judiciary, enforcement (as already indicated), and fiscal relations such as taxation (Kottak 2013, 391-397; Sharma and Gupta 2006). His definition has problems but does express the major characteristic of a state well.

CHAPTER TWENTY-ONE

Origins and Evolution of Ideological Diversity: Religious Identity

Introduction

- Mythology: the discourse of religion, the narrative of religion.
- Religion: a system of beliefs and practices directed toward the ultimate concern of society.
- For Emile Durkheim (2001), religious beliefs "are the representations which express the nature of sacred things and the relations which they sustain, either with each other or with profane things."
- Durkheim (2001) continues: "Rites are the rules of conduct which prescribe how a 'man' should comport himself in the presence of these sacred objects."
- Religion is made of two fundamental categories—beliefs and rites.
- There are two domains in religion—the sacred and the profane.

- For Max Weber (1963 [1922]), religion is a social institution of definite procedure and fixed dogma.

- Cosmology: explanations of the world in which a person and group lives and their place in that world; the meaning of the world.
- Space
- Time
- The meaning of the human condition
- Human constitution
- Human growth and creativity

- Eschatology: death and the end of time.
- Many religions have strong views about what happens upon death of the individual and what happens at the end of time (when the world as we know it comes to an end).

The Praxis of Religion: Witches, Shamans, Sorceresses, Priests, and Prophets

Witchcraft

- A psychic power
- Often hereditary
- May be unconscious

Sorcery

- Use of medicines toward an evil end
- Anyone can learn it
- Conscious

Explanation of Witchcraft

- Witchcraft as an explanation of misfortune.

- Witchcraft provides some action, which may be taken to alleviate these misfortunes.
- Witchcraft brings social tensions out into the open.
- Witchcraft has a normative effect on society (see Siegel 2006; Rosenthal and Siegel 1959):
    1. To avoid being accused of witchcraft.
    2. To avoid incurring the wrath of a witch.

- Example of use of hallucinogens: St. Anthony's fire (Ergot, *Claviceps purpurea*): a parasite of cereals, particularly rye. A case of massive intoxication, thought to be a plague of "holy fire" in Europe in 1039. The cause was not discovered until 1676 (Schultes and Hofmann 1992).

Shaman and Shamanism

- Shaman (witch-doctor): comparative studies by M. Eliade (1978, 1952).
- Weber's (1963 [1922]) *the magician*; individual, self-employed.
- Shamanism: based on the definition of Siberian shamanism.
- A shaman is an individual that through ecstasies and possession is able to act as an intermediary in communication with the spirits.

Use of Hallucinogens

- Mushrooms and the Finno-Ugrian shamans of Siberia.
- Example: Fly Agaric (*Amanita muscaria*), one of the oldest known hallucinogens and, once perhaps, the most widely used (Schultes and Hofmann 1992).
- Example: a Finno-Ugrian shaman-priestess in a ritual trance dance in Siberia (Schultes and Hofmann 1992).

- Cactus: Peyote (*Opuntia* sp., *Lophophora williamsii*) used by the Huichol shaman of Mexico (Schultes and Hofmann 1992).

- Vines: Ayahuasca (*Banisteriopsis caapi*) used by Western Amazonian shamans.
- Makuna Indians cultivate the *caapi* liana, although wild plants are preferred (Schultes and Raffauf 1990).
- Example: a Barasana medicine man lighting the pitch-torch to signal the beginning of a *caapi* ceremony (Schultes and Raffauf 1990).

- Shamanism is only present as an all-embracing system in non-centralized societies. Therefore, shamanism is generally considered to be elementary as a symbolic system or form of religion.
- Shamanistic phenomena are also found in centralized societies, which points to the adaptive character of shamanism. Its manifestations in centralized societies are not only fragmentary and altered, but peripheral or even opposed to the central authorities.
- Shamanic practices in all types of society become manifest, especially in periods of crisis, when such practices easily revive or emerge. Shamanism, as such, is not found in the position of a state religion.

Institutionalized Religion: Prophet, Priest, and the Priesthood

- The prophet: power based on personal revelations and charisma; founder of religions; her/his mission is doctrine. Prophets often practice divination, as well as magical healing and counseling.
- The priest: functionaries of a regularly organized and permanent enterprise concerned with influencing the gods. With permanent places of fixed cult centers. The doctrine is also fixed.
- The sacred: From Latin *sacer*, set off, restricted, to be of the domain of priesthood.

Nineteenth to Twentieth Century Explanations on the Origins of Religion

- Animism: Edward B. Tylor (1871); the main question was how humans created the concept of the soul. He argued that the concept was universal and originated in the human effort to interpret dreams. The belief in Spiritual beings is the minimum definition of religion that Tylor proposed. He also proposed an evolution by stages of religion in the sequence: animism, polydaemonism, polytheism, and finally monotheism.
- Magic: James Frazer's (1911–1915 [1890]) view of magic as a "false science". An age of magic preceded an age of religion. The common factor between imitative (homeopathic magic) and contagious magic (contact magic) is the sympathetic principle: like to like, or similar things, are somehow capable of influencing each other.
- Totemism: a cult to the ancestors. The totem represents the clan. Totems become objects of a cult, because they represent the society; the totem is virtually god. A totem is an animal or plant used as a symbol or emblem of the clan. The notion of a supreme being depends on the totemic belief.

The Source of Religious Variation

- Religious movements
- Revitalization movements
- Millennial cults and messianic movements

Main Institutionalized Religions of the World

- Christian religions: Catholicism, Protestantism, Orthodox
- Judaism
- Islam
- Buddhism
- Hinduism
- Taoism
- Confucianism
- Shinto sects

The Diversity of Rituals

Categorization of Rituals Prior to Arnold van Gennep (French Ethnographer and Folklorist [1873–1957])

- Animistic rites
- Dynamistic rites
- Sympathetic rites
- Contagious rites
- Positive rites
- Negative rites

- Animistic Rites: rituals based on the personalistic theory of power in a single or multiple being, animal or plant (e.g., totem), anthropomorphic or amorphous (e.g. God).
- Dynamistic Rites: rituals based on the impersonal theory of Mana. Mana is a concept that originated in Melanesia. It is a form of supernatural power that is not physical, not fixed in anything but capable of being conveyed in almost anything. It is impersonal, non-anthropomorphized.
- Sympathetic Rites: related to homeopathic magic, based on similarity or imitation.
- Contagious Rites: related to contagious magic, based on contact.
- Positive rites based on the idea of positive magic or sorcery
- Negative rites based on the idea of negative magic or Taboo

Van Gennep's Proposal in Terms of Rites of Passage (2004 [1908])

- Rites of separation: Preliminal rites
- Transition rites: Liminal rites
- Rites of incorporation: Postliminal rites

Categorization of Rituals of Passage

- Territorial passage
- Neutral grounds: buffer zone
- Purification
- Portal rituals

- Individual and group passages are the domain of incorporation rites
- Pregnancy and childbirth passage
- Birth and childhood passage

- Initiation rites of passage: physiological puberty, social puberty, betrothal and marriage passage

- Funeral ceremonies are the domain of rites of separation
- Rites of the first time
- Rites of appropriation

Victor Turner and the Anthropology of Performance, Theater, and Ritual

- Victor Turner (1920–1983): British Cultural Anthropologist known for work on symbolic and interpretive Anthropology. Publications: *From Ritual to Theatre: The Human Seriousness of Play* (1982), *Dramas, Fields, and Metaphors: Symbolic Action in Humans* (1974), and *The Forest of Symbols: Aspects of Ndembu Ritual* (1967).

- Ritual: a prescribed formal behavior for occasions not given over to technological routine, having reference to beliefs in invisible beings or powers, regarded as the first and final causes of all effects.

Ritual as Performance

- The term "performance" is derived from Old English *parfournir*, literally "to furnish completely or thoroughly." To perform is thus to bring something about, to consummate something, or to carry out a play, order, or project.
- The importance of liminal rituals in tribal and agrarian societies. Typical of mechanical solidarity.
- Liminoid or leisure genres of symbolic forms and action in complex industrial societies.
- Typical of organic solidarity.

Social Dramas and Stage Dramas

- The Greek term "drama" means a "deed" or "act." Act is applied to the action represented on stage. Social dramas are narratives. Social dramas are the "raw stuff," out of which theater comes and out of which a drama is continually regenerated, to be created as societies develop in scale and complexity.

- Social dramas can be subdivided in preliterate societies into:
  1. Sickness or misfortunes
  2. Crisis, recourse to divine, or oracular procedures
  3. Remedial ritual action
  4. Ritual cooperation

CHAPTER TWENTY-TWO

Introduction to Economic Anthropology

Approaches of Economic Anthropology

1. Formalist approach
2. Substantivist approach
3. Marxist approach or production theory

1. Formalist Approach

- Melville Herskovits (1895–1963), an American anthropologist who helped establish African and African-American studies at universities in the U.S. Publications: *Economic Anthropology: A Study in Comparative Economics* (1952) and *The Economic Life of Primitive Peoples* (1940).
- Use of the neoclassic view of economy proposed by Adam Smith (1776). Rational action is the key in economic decisions.
- Use of the concepts: supply, demand, and price.
- Scarcity of resources: the assumption that resources will never be plentiful enough for people to obtain all the goods they desire.

2. Substantivist Approach

- Marshall Sahlins (1930–Present): American anthropologist. Publication: *Stone Age Economics* (1972).

- Karl Polanyi (1886–1964): economic historian. Publication: *The Great Transformation* (1944).

Forms of Economic Integration

- Reciprocity: the exchange of goods and services of equal value.

- Exchange:
  1. Generalized: those who exchange do so without expecting an immediate return and without specifying the value of the return.
  2. Balanced: exchange done in equal terms or values.
  3. Negative: exchange where one party seeks a profit in the relationship.

- Redistribution: a form of exchange that demands a centralized social organization to receive the economic contribution of the members of the group and to redistribute them when they are needed to the members of the group by their chief or by the main authority of the group. Example: Potlatch in the northwest coast of North America.
- Market exchange: The exchange of goods (trade) calculated in terms of a multipurpose medium of exchange and standard of value (money).

3. Marxist Approach or Production Theory

- Karl Marx (1818–1883), German philosopher and economist. Publications: *The Communist Manifesto* (1848, with Friedrich Engels, originally published in German) and *Capital* (1867, originally published in German).

- Labor: The activity linking human social groups to the material world of production.
- Means of production: The tools, or means, to produce materials or goods.
- Modes of production: A characterization of the relationship between the labor, the means of production, and who controls the means of production. Examples: feudal, capitalist, primitive communist, and socialist mode of production.

- Feudalism: the economic and social system of Medieval Europe, in which land worked by serfs was held by vassals who provided military and other services to overlords.

- Communism: a social order where private property is abolished, and all things are equally held or controlled by the members of the community. Primitive communism is more in line with the idea that the means of production and distribution are not privately owned but are controlled by the corporate, self-perpetuating kinship group.

- Socialism: a theory or scheme of social order that places the means of production and distribution in the hands of the community.

- Capitalism: the economic system where the means of production and distribution are privately owned.

- According to Karl Marx, the contradiction between the owner of (or who controls) the means of production and labor creates the different modes of production, and the conflict between the two generates changes from one mode of production to the next one.

Phases of Economic Life

- Production: the transformation of raw materials into a form suitable to be consumed.
- Distribution: the allocation of goods and services.
- Consumption: the use of material goods.

Other Concepts

- Formal economy: the exchange of goods under the rules of the town, state, or nation. They are usually subject to a form of direct or indirect taxation or tribute.
- Informal economy: the illegal activities of an economic nature that are not under the political control of the town, state, or nation. Example: the mafia and the street sellers in Latin America.
- Conspicuous Consumption: Concept developed by Thorstein Veblen (1857–1929) in *The Theory of the Leisure Class* (1899). Material goods that are consumed, because they give prestige or status, not because they are necessary.

Gift Exchange: An Example of Generalized Exchange

- Marcel Mauss (1872–1950), French sociologist. Publications include *The Gift: Forms and Functions of Exchange in Archaic Societies* (1966 [1925]).
    1. The obligation to give
    2. The obligation to receive
    3. The obligation to repay

- Examples used by Mauss (1966 [1925]):
    1. The Kula: a system of gift-giving in the Trobriand Islands. *Soulava:* necklaces. *Mwali:* armbands. Purpose of the Kula: ensures communication and creates a social network between the islands.
    2. The Mana, the case of the Maori and Samoa. Gifts have some mana. This is passed through the forms of *Taonga*, which can be property, labor or merchandise. This power can destroy the recipient of a gift if it is not repaid. The purpose is to create spiritual obligations.
    3. The Potlatch: a form of competitive feasting where gifts play a role in creating obligations by the receiver of the gifts.

The Gift after Mauss

- Levi-Strauss: view of exchange.
- Exchange in marriage:
    1. Restricted or direct exchange
    2. Generalized or indirect exchange

Examples of Generalized and Balanced Exchange: Hunter-Gatherers, Horticulturalists, and Pastoralists

- Why is negative exchange for profit less likely to occur in these societies?

- Hunter-gatherers:
    1. Highly mobile. Material necessities are limited following the axiom "want not, lack not."
    2. Mode of production is geared toward self-sufficiency and not surplus production. Studies suggest they spend a mean of three to five hours per adult

per day in food production (Lee 1979; Sahlins 1968). Material possessions are not an incentive to work harder (you cannot take them with you anyway).

3. Risk management strategies involve food sharing or the concept of "the gift"—to give, to receive, and to repay in a form of social obligation.

4. Production and exchange focus on the use value of the object. This value can be looked at, in essence, as how useful an object is to the individual or group. The accumulation of more than one or two objects of a type is not useful.

- Using Marxist terms, where C is the commodity, and M is the medium of exchange such as, for instance, money or the actual exchange: C - M - C. In this case, the objective is to obtain C and not the medium of exchange, M.

- Horticulturalists and pastoralists:
- This type of exchange also occurs in horticultural/pastoral societies as both generalized and balanced exchange. Here, we see the development of bartering systems, again, with the objective to obtain useful products or use value.

- With the advent of larger distance trade networks, markets, and the development of symbolic mediums of exchange (i.e., money), exchange can be seen as negative or for a profit.

- In this case, M - C - M where the objective is to obtain more of the medium of exchange or the exchange value.

- Here, the focus is on obtaining more of the medium of exchange, where M equals infinity. This process necessitates the creation of a concept of scarcity to keep prices high and demand high in terms of "want more, lack more, buy more."

- It appears to be that the shift to negative exchange creates this cycle, which is lacking in hunter-gatherers and many horticultural and pastoralist societies that utilize group and kinship relations to secure "social wealth" as an economic/ideological strategy of success.

CHAPTER TWENTY-THREE

A Brief History of the Industrial Revolution: Population, Technology, and Economics

Introduction

- Information for this chapter was compiled from Braudel (1981 [1979]).

- Estimated populations in the Old World in the fifteenth to eighteenth centuries.
- No one knows the total population of the world between the 15th and 18th centuries.
- In Western Europe, a prolonged population rise occurred between AD 1100 and 1350, another between AD 1450 and 1650, and a third after AD 1750. Sharp decreases occurred between AD 1350 and 1450 due to disease (the Black Death) and again from AD 1650 to 1750 (Braudel 1981, 39).

- Estimated European population is between 250 and 350 million in AD 1300 and probably doubled by AD 1780.
- The extraordinary demographic increase in China occurs around AD 1680 with ca. 120 million people up to AD 1850 with ca. 430 million people.
- A revolution in agricultural technologies is cited as the cause for this demographic increase
- "A growing increase in the number of people often ends, and always ended in the past, by exceeding the capacity of the society concerned to feed them" (Braudel 1981, 33).
- This need to feed more people caused by population pressure is seen by Boserup (1965) as the driving force behind the invention of new technologies.

- These new technologies are applied initially to agriculture, which can lead to further population growth.
- Boserup (1965) indicates that increased populations result in the shift from horticultural to extensive agricultural (slash and burn) societies. As population continues to rise in a given area, extensive agricultural practices shift to intensive ones (intensive agricultural societies) where new technologies (i.e., the plow, irrigation, fertilization, machinery) are invented to increase the carrying capacity of a particular area or territory.
- The term "Industrial Revolution" refers to the dramatic technological and economic innovations that occurred in England during the period from about AD 1760 to 1830.
- Definition in Nolan and Lenski (2006, 193): "To be meaningful, the term should be limited to the period during which the productive activities of societies were rapidly transformed by the invention of a succession of machines powered by newer, inanimate sources of energy, such as coal, electricity, petroleum, and natural gas."
- The basic cause was the growing store of technological information in the latter part of the agrarian era (i.e., prior to the 1700s).
- The spread of new technological and ideological information was increased by the development of the printing press, which was a system of movable type, probably invented by Johann Gutenberg in the middle of the 15th century (1400s).

First Phase

- Textile machines. The traditional spinning wheel was replaced by the spinning jenny. This lead to large looms that could not be operated by humans.
- A demand for alternative sources of energy led to the invention of steam engines by James Watt.
- These inventions led to the rapid expansion of the British textile industries between AD 1770 and 1845.
- One of the immediate consequences of the advances in textile production was the creation of a factory system.
- Production was no longer controlled at the household or community level, but control shifted to the owners of the machines and factories.

- Indicative of three clear characteristics of capitalism or an economic system where the means of production and distribution are privately owned.
    1. Means of production controlled outside of the household and community by owners of machines and factories
    2. Means of distribution controlled outside the household and community by a merchant class that owns the transportation to take products to distant locations
    3. Payment required is not in the form of useful goods but as a set exchange medium or money, whereby the goal of the exchange is not balanced (one useful product for another), but is for more money than was initially paid for the product or, in other words, for profit.

- Iron use also expanded greatly in this first phase, thanks to the invention of the coal-fired blast furnace. For instance in AD 1788, England produced 68,000 tons of iron; by AD 1845 this had increased 24 times.

Second Phase

- One of the most important developments was the use of the steam engine for transportation, leading to large networks of railroads and steamships.
- This allowed for the contact and opening up of new markets for the products being produced in England and Europe.
- "It is only a step from market to colony" (Braudel 1981, 102).

- Colonialism: the political, social, economic, and cultural domination of a territory and its people by a foreign power for an extended time.
- Modern colonialism began with the "Age of Discovery," during which European nations founded colonies throughout the New World. An early phase occurred from AD 1492 to 1825, and a more imperialistic phase ran from AD 1850 to just after the end of World War II.

- Other important technological innovations include in the rubber industry with vulcanization, which prevented rubber goods from becoming sticky in hot weather.

- In the 1860s, the electric dynamo was invented, which allowed for the large scale use of electricity in industry, and the transformer was invented, which helped to alleviate the loss of energy during long-distance transmissions.
- A hierarchy of salaried managers within industries also began.

Third Phase

- The early 1900s brought a new phase to the Industrial Revolution, particularly in the fields of transportation, electricity, and communications.
- Discoveries in the late 1800s by inventors, like Thomas Edison, allowed for the development of new industries. These inventions include the internal combustion engine (automobiles), telephone, radio, moving pictures, electric generator, and plastics.

- The common denominator in all these inventions was the focus on the individual.
- These technological innovations allowed the individual to:
  1. Have access to more services
  2. Have more decision-making powers on how to spend the money earned by selling his/her labor
  3. Be pulled into the market economy by creating the individual's need (demand) for more products

Fourth Phase

- The Information Age: Technological innovations that have increased the individual's access to information.
- The main innovations include computers, television, transistors, the Internet, and plastics.
- Television is especially important as a device to affect individuals' belief systems, since the actions of vast numbers of people who watch TV can be manipulated by its content, though this is debated.

Examples of Wealthiest World Nations Since the 1880s

- In 1888, 83% of the world's industrial output occurred in five societies: the United States, Britain, Germany, France, and Russia.
- In 2003, these societies accounted for only 46%, with Japan ranked second in gross domestic product (Nolan and Lenski 2006, 2002).
- GDP: gross domestic product and is a measure of the value of all of the goods and services produced in a society.
- In 2012, the United States, China, Japan, Germany, and France held the highest-estimated gross domestic product of any other countries in the world.

Table 23.1. Ranking of Economies of Countries by Estimated GDP in 2012 from the World Development Indicators Database, World Bank, 17 December 2013

Ranking	Economy	Millions of US Dollars
1	United States	16,244,600
2	China	8,227,103
3	Japan	5,959,718
4	Germany	3,428,131
5	France	2,612,878
6	United Kingdom	2,471,784
7	Brazil	2,252,664
8	Russian Federation	2,014,775
9	Italy	2,014,670
10	India	1,841,710
11	Canada	1,821,424
12	Australia	1,532,408
13	Spain	1,322,965
14	Mexico	1,178,126
15	Korea, Rep.	1,129,598
16	Indonesia	878,043
17	Turkey	789,257
18	Netherlands	770,555
19	Saudi Arabia	711,050
20	Switzerland	631,173

CHAPTER TWENTY-FOUR

Industrial Societies: Ideologies and Politics

The Continued Importance of the Individual

1. Breakdown of kinship structures
2. Development of private property versus communal property
3. Stress of the individual in religious ideologies
4. Stress of the individual in political and secular ideologies

1. Breakdown of Kinship Structures

- The location of production moves from the household and local community to some outside location not associated with kinship.
- Lineage and clan affiliations become less important, as access to resources is attained through the acquisition of wealth (i.e., money).
- In industrialized societies, this can occur at the level of the individual.

2. Development of Private Property versus Communal Property

- In non-industrial societies (i.e., band and horticultural/ pastoral groups), access to resources is controlled at the communal level by lineage and clan affiliations.
- In industrial societies, as the importance of mechanized means of production increases, so does the shift to individual ownership of resources.
- This can be viewed as a shift to private property, where individuals own the means of production.

- The first phase of the Industrial Revolution.
- One of the immediate consequences of the advances in textile production was the creation of a factory system.
- Production was no longer controlled at the household or community level, but control shifted to the owners of the machines and factories.
- This process is indicative of three clear characteristics of capitalism or an economic system where the means of production and distribution are privately owned.
    1. Means of production controlled outside of the household and community by owners of machines and factories
    2. Means of distribution controlled outside the household and community by a merchant class that owns the transportation to take products to distant locations
    3. Payment required is not in the form of useful goods, but as a set exchange medium or money whereby the goal of the exchange is not balanced (one useful product for another) but is for more money than was initially paid for the product or, in other words, for profit

3. Stress of the Individual in Religious Ideologies

- The great historical faiths were developed during the agrarian era. These include Judaism, Christianity, Islam, Hinduism, and Buddhism.
- In particular in Christianity, these included the need of the masses to communicate to God through some intermediary (i.e., priest).

- With the Protestant Reformation and the teachings of Martin Luther, the individual was seen as an important element in religion.
- Thanks to the invention of movable type (the printing press) in the 1400s, these teachings could reach large groups of people.
- "The Protestant doctrine of the priesthood of all believers—the doctrine that all believers are equal in God's sight and can relate directly to Him without the mediation of the clergy" (Nolan and Lenski 2006, 244).
- The individual was, thus, seen as a viable force in the interpretation of the Bible and in the control of his/her own destiny.
- These teachings changed humans' views toward work and wealth accumulation leading toward industrialization and capitalism.

- Also see the work of Max Weber (1930 [1904–1905, 1920]).
    1. Work is an important form of service to God.
    2. The Protestant faiths undermined fatalism and a trust in magic and stimulated the spread in rationalism.
    3. The teachings stressed the value of frugal living, allowing for those that were economically successful to accumulate capital and that this could be seen as a justifiable goal in itself.

Conflicts Between This Individualistic View and Other Agrarian Faiths

- Example: Fundamentalist Islam (or other fundamentalist religious sects) seems to reject most of the values on which economic growth and development depend.
    a. Education for the masses is limited to religious texts and might not include information necessary for technological development. Education in industrialized societies is public, is non-religious, and includes the sciences.
    b. An acceptance of the conditions of the world is stressed, and true fulfillment will occur in the afterlife. Conditions in this world are far less important than attainment of Paradise in the afterlife. Industrial societies search for improvements to today's conditions through technological means.
    c. Governments should be controlled by religious leaders and not secular entities. Their decrees are believed to have the authority of God behind them. Most governments of industrialized societies are now secular, shifting away, for instance, from monarchies governed by hereditary kings and queens whose powers were seen to be vested in God (see map of political systems from Allen and Shalinsky 2004).
    d. Modern means of birth control are considered sinful, and large families are required, as would be necessary in agrarian or pre-industrial societies. Industrial societies (1.6 total fertility rate [TFR]) have much lower fertility rates than non-industrial societies (3.1 TFR, see Table 13.2, Nolan and Lenski 2006, 274)(TFR is an estimate of the number of children the average woman will have in her lifetime)(see map on total fertility rate, 1990–2000 from Allen and Shalinsky 2004).
    e. All who do not share the same view are looked upon with hostility. Industrial societies are often comprised of varying ethnic, religious, civic, and other groups.

4. Stress of the Individual in Secular Ideologies and Polities

- A number of trends in secular ideologies and politics has occurred since the Industrial Revolution.
- These include capitalism, democratic republicanism, oligarchical republicanism, socialism, democratic socialism, revolutionary socialism (communism), nationalism, pragmatism, and hedonism.

The Trend Toward Democracy

- Democracy: a form of government in which the supreme power in retained by the people collectively and exercised directly or indirectly through their representatives. Government by the people and for the people. Important aspect: "the exercise of the powers of government to benefit the masses of ordinary people in countless ways" (Nolan and Lenski 2006, 242).
- Plutocracy: governments run by the rich.
- Causes for the increase of democracies around the world:
  a. The Protestant Reformation and "the doctrine that all believers are equal in God's sight and can relate directly to Him without the mediation of the clergy" (Nolan and Lenski 2006, 244). From the United States Declaration of Independence (1776): "We hold these truths to be self-evident, that *all men are created equal*, that they are endowed by their Creator with certain unalienable Rights, that among these are Life, Liberty and the pursuit of Happiness" (italics added by author)(http://www.archives.gov/exhibits/charters/declaration_transcript.html). These ideas underlie the concept of basic human rights, as well (http://www.un.org/en/documents/udhr/history.shtml).
  b. The conquest of the New World opened up areas where the equality of individuals could be developed, in governmental form, away from already institutionalized forms of monarchy (i.e., England, France, Spain, and Russia).
  c. Industrialization required a more skilled and educated working class. Education allows people to question "authority." "Knowledge is power."

Political Conflict and Stability

- Democracies in industrial societies have tended to be stable forms of political control for numerous reasons.

1. Their greater productivity and higher standard of living give the majority of people a vested interest in political stability.

2. A democratic ideology strengthens individuals' affiliations to their governments in opposition to revolutionary movements.

3. The complexity of the structure of industrial societies promotes compromise. Many people occur in intermediary positions between contending parties.

4. Each individual simultaneously fills a number of different roles or identities and belongs to different groups (political, religious, ethnic, class). Therefore, one does not always find herself/himself on the opposing side of all issues from other individuals in other groups.

Table 24.1. The General Components Involved in the Development of Complex Societies

Type of Society	Hunter-Gatherer/ Foraging	Horticulture/ Pastoral	Agrarian	Industrial
Population	- Small - ca. 50-100 people	- Medium - ca. 5,000-10,000 people or more	- Large - Over 10,000 to hundreds of thousands people	- Large - Hundreds of thousands of people or more
Culture	- Group identity markers	- Group identity and territorial markers - Ideologies of cults to the ancestors	- Group identity and territorial markers - Status differentiation - Ideological group markers	- Nationalism - Ethnic groups
Material Products	-Rudimentary -Stone/Plant tools	-Rudimentary -Stone/Plant tools	- Plow - Milling devices - Metallurgy	- Industrial machines - Non-renewable energy sources

Table 24.1. The General Components Involved in the Development of Complex Societies

Type of Society	Hunter-Gatherer/ Foraging	Horticulture/ Pastoral	Agrarian	Industrial
Energy Source	- Human	- Human -Animal	- Human - Animal - Minimal machines (water/wind)	- Machines - Non-renewable energy sources - Human/ animal
Control of Production	-Nuclear family (household)	-Nuclear family (household) - Kinship Linkages	-Nuclear family (household) - Kinship Linkages - Owner of land (Hereditary)	- Owners of machines/ factories
Location of Production	- Home territory	- Household - Village Territory	- Household - Community Territory (Cottage Industries)	- Factories outside of home and community
Exchange Mechanism	- Generalized	- Generalized - Balanced (barter)	- Generalized - Balanced (barter) between communities - Development of negative exchange & a merchant class	- Negative (profit motive) - Merchant class controls transportation
Payment for Labor	- "The gift"	- "The gift" - higher status - other products	- "The gift" - higher status - other products	- Money
Status	- Egalitarian - Achieved status	- Ranked based on prestige - Achieved status - Start of ascribed status	- Stratified based on wealth, power, and prestige/ status - Ascribed/ Achieved - Classes/ Castes	- Stratified based on wealth, power, and prestige/ status -Often focused on wealth accumulation

Socio-Economic

Table 24.1. The General Components Involved in the Development of Complex Societies

Type of Society	Hunter-Gatherer/ Foraging	Horticulture/ Pastoral	Agrarian	Industrial
Social-Political Institutions	- Kinship - Band - Extended Family - Social mechanisms of behavior control	- Kinship - Tribe - Lineages and clans - Social/ ideological mechanisms of behavior control, arbitration	- Chiefdoms and States - Theocracies/ Nobility (ruler believed to be a God) - Rule-centered legal codes	- Shift toward democracies+ individual human rights
Political Institutions	- Band - Egalitarian	-Tribal -Ranking - Development of chiefdoms	- Chiefdoms - Development of states - Stratification	- States - Stratification
Religious Ideologies	- Animism	- Animism - Magic - Totemism (ancestor worship)	- Totemism (ancestor worship) - Development of monotheism/ polytheism	- Monotheism - Polytheism

CHAPTER TWENTY-FIVE

Gender Relations

Introduction

- *Sex* refers to biological differences, while *gender* refers to cultural constructions of male and female characteristics.
- Sexual dimorphism: the marked differences in male and female biology.
- Gender roles: the tasks and activities that a culture gives to the sexes.
- Gender stereotypes: oversimplified but strongly engrained ideas of the characteristics of men and women.
- Gender stratification describes an unequal distribution of wealth, power, and status or prestige between men and women and reflects their different positions in a particular social hierarchy.

Sex-Linked Activities

- Three possible theories (see Kottak 2013, Tables 18.1 through 18.4):
  1. Compatibility-with-child-care theory:
- Women's tasks tend to be those that are compatible with childcare.
- For instance, lactation and pregnancy tend to preclude the possibility of women being the primary hunters in foraging societies, which would keep them away from the home (base) for longer periods of time and at greater distances (see Binford 2001, 238).

- In industrial societies, women are still the main caregivers.
  2. Economy-of-effort theory:
- It is more advantageous, in terms of expendable energy, for one gender to perform a set of tasks that are related in some manner (i.e., males to make musical instruments, because they collect the raw materials for the instruments; if women are located closer to home, it is more efficient for them to perform duties related to the home).
  3. Expendability theory:
- Men will do more dangerous tasks and go to war, because they are more expendable in that the loss of men is less reproductively disadvantageous than the loss of women.
- Almost universally in the past, the greater size, strength, and mobility of men have led to their exclusive service in the roles of hunters and warriors.

Sexuality and Gender

- Sexual orientation
- All human activities, including sexual preferences, are, to some extent, learned and malleable.
- Sexual orientation refers to a person's habitual sexual attractions and activities.

- Heterosexuality: attracted to persons of the opposite sex.
- Homosexuality: attracted to persons of the same sex.
- Bisexuality: attracted to persons from both sexes.
- Asexuality: indifference or lack of attraction to either sex.

- Sexual norms vary considerably cross culturally and through time.
- Example: Ritualized homosexual behavior among the Etoro of Papua New Guinea, as well as up to 50 other tribes in the region (Kelly 1976; Kottak 2013, 418–421).
- Etoro culture is used as an example of extreme sexual antagonism and the degree to which gender roles are culturally constructed.
- Pregnancies are believed to be caused by an ancestral spirit, and semen nourishes the fetus but also saps the man of vital life force, leading to female–male sexual taboos.
- Insemination of young male initiates by older males is viewed as a moral obligation, while heterosexual intercourse is severely restricted by taboos. Males are believed

to not be able to produce semen on their own, which has to be obtained initially from older men orally.

Gender Stratification

- Strong differentiation between the home and the outside world is called the domestic-public dichotomy, or the private-public contrast.
- Gender status tends to be more equal when there is not a sharp separation between these two domains, as is the case with foragers.
- Roughly equal contributions to subsistence by men and women correlates with lower stratification.
- As women's contribution to subsistence becomes differentially high or low, gender stratification increases.
- Gender stratification is lower when domestic and public spheres are not clearly distinguished.
- Further, one must think of stratification as having three dimensions: wealth, power, and prestige or status, and these are more clearly demarcated in complex state-level societies (Weber 1922 [1968]). In less complex societies, such as bands, tribes, and chiefdoms, initial kinship group ranking usually occurs based on prestige.
- One must remember that, in many non-industrial societies, it is the rank or prestige of the kinship group (lineage or clan, for instance) that determines the relative status of both men and women in the society. These can be referred to as *ancestor-focused* societies (Fox 1967, 163–164; Goodenough 1951).
- In industrial societies (*ego-focused*), the individual is the focus, not the kinship group as a corporate entity (perpetuated through time); and, it is the actual individual, male or female, whose status and attendant wealth and power is situated in the social hierarchy of the society.
- All of these factors must be considered when determining why a particular sex, male or female, has a particular status (prestige), wealth, or power in a given society.

Gender Stratification among Foragers (Bands)

- Foraging, or hunter-gatherer, societies are comprised of nuclear families that temporarily come together to form a band.
- This structure could allow these societies to be defined as ego-focused, and each individual's contribution to subsistence helps determine his or her status and power with little wealth accumulation.
- With foragers or bands, gender status tends to be more equal, since there is not a sharp contrast between the private and public domains and, generally, men and women both contribute equally to the subsistence of the group.

Gender Stratification among Horticultural and Pastoral Tribal Societies

- Tribal societies are generally comprised of lineages and clans, which are ancestor focused. The kinship group is the self-perpetuating entity, and these are often, though not always, ranked in terms of prestige. As they become more complex, power and wealth differentiations can also be seen.
- As such, the individual's particular position in the society is often based on the kinship group to which he or she belongs.

- In matrilineal, uxorilocal societies, gender stratification is reduced, or men and women often have equal status.
- Further, female status tends to be relatively high in matrilineal, uxorilocal societies (e.g., Iroquois).
- Reasons for high female status are that women had economic power due to inheritance, and the residence pattern lent itself to female solidarity. They also contribute a great deal to the subsistence of the group.
- While matriarchal societies are now believed to be non-existent, the Iroquois are an example of virtually equal status for men and women in a horticultural society from an ego-focused point of view.

- In patrilineal-virilocal societies, there is increased gender stratification.
- In this case, since women do not inherit property, wealth etc. and leave their natal home, female status is dependent on the status of her husband and his kinship group.

- This arrangement is still ancestor focused, but taken from the point of view of a focus on ego or the individual, there is increased gender stratification as the female, alone, has no recourse to title, land, power, or wealth.

- This combination tends to enhance male prestige opportunities and result in relatively high gender stratification (e.g., societies in the highland of Papua-New Guinea).
- The spread of patrilineal-virilocal societies has been associated with pressure on resources and increased local warfare.

Patriarchy and Violence

- The male role in warfare is highly valued.
- Violent acts against women are common and include dowry murders, female infanticide, and clitoridectomies.

- Domestic violence. Family violence is a worldwide problem.
- Abuse of women is more common in societies where women are separated from their supportive kin ties (e.g., patrilineal, patrifocal, virilocal, and neolocal societies).

Gender Stratification among Agriculturalists (Chiefdoms and Pre-Industrial States)

- Again in chiefdoms and pre-industrial states, the societies are organized based on kinship, and one's access to prestige, wealth, and power can be determined by the position one was born into upon birth (ascribed status). This would be regardless of whether one is male or female.
- In these more complex societies, stratification in terms not only of status or prestige, but wealth and power can be identified (i.e., castes).
- When viewing stratification from an ego-focus, there is some tendency for agriculture to accentuate gender stratification, since the heavier labor involved is usually done by men, which reduces the economic power of women.
- However, there are many exceptions, where women still do most of the cultivation work and have a correspondingly high status.

Gender Stratification in Industrial, State-Level Societies

- In many industrial, state-level societies, the nuclear family and neolocal residence patterns are the norm. Along with the development of the division of labor, ego-focused relations are typical.
- In these circumstances, it is the individual and not the larger kinship group that is situated in a society based on the stratification of prestige, wealth, and power.
- In general, gender stratification is higher and women's status viewed as lower when the public-domestic dichotomy is stronger (women are "just" housewives), or if men lose their jobs, their status is also viewed as being lower.
- As females have entered the workforce by leaving home, their access to wealth, power, and status has increased, though gaps still exist between men and women in terms of income/wages and holding positions of power.
- Since World War II, the number of women in the work force has increased dramatically, driven in large part by industries' search for cheap, educated labor in combination with technology mitigating the effect of notions about appropriate work for women.

The Feminization of Poverty

- In many industrial societies, the nuclear family has disappeared, and we see many minimal nuclear units, or the mother and offspring. These arrangements are often clearly ego-focused in that the individual parent has the sole responsibility for subsistence for the family unit.
- In fact, the number of single-parent, female-headed households has doubled since 1959, with the largest proportion of these being minorities.
- The combination of dual responsibilities (parenting and work) and poorer employment opportunities means that these households are increasingly poverty stricken.
- In these situations, gender stratification is obviously high, as females have limited access to wealth and power and are viewed (at least in the past) with having lower status than males.

CHAPTER TWENTY-SIX

Order and War

This chapter deals with four related topics, as follows:

1. Rules and norms
2. Sanctions
3. Disputes and conflict resolution
4. War

1. Rules and Norms

Norms

- Norm: *a statement of rule that is indigenously regarded as relevant to the regulation of social conduct.*
- Norms are acceptable forms of behavior that are considered normal. Anything that departs from that normality is unacceptable to the group.

Rules

- Rules: defined norms. When the rules are not accepted by an individual, his/her actions are considered to be against the group that defined the rule. As a consequence, a social control method, such as a sanction, will usually occur.

2. Sanctions

- Alfred Reginald Radcliffe-Brown (1881–1955)(British Social Anthropologist) defined sanctions as a reaction on the part of a society or of a considerable number of its members to a mode of behavior which is thereby approved (positive sanctions) or disapproved (negative sanctions).
- Publications include: *Structure and Function in Primitive Societies* (1952) and *The Andaman Islanders* (1933).

Negative Sanctions

- Negative sanctions: forms of penalties for breaking a rule. These can only be employed through direct punishment or indirect punishment. There are other minor forms of sanctions, such as gossip, avoidance, and ridicule, within a group.

Positive Sanctions

- Positive sanctions: rewards, such as increases in prestige or status or prizes.

Organized Sanctions

- Organized sanctions: typical of large-scale groups and relate to a clear legal system of sanctions.

Diffuse Sanctions

- Diffuse sanctions: typical of small-scale societies where forms of social pressure are effective, such as gossip, ostracism, satirical behavior, or public mockery.

Other Forms of Sanctions

- Radcliffe-Brown also defined religious and ritual sanctions in relation to ideology.
- Economic sanctions.

3. Disputes and Conflict Resolution

- There are two different ways to analyze dispute settlement: rule centered and processual.

1. Rule centered: law should be seen as "principles extracted from legal decisions."
   - Under the rule-centered paradigm a law can be seen under the following terms: A social norm is legal if its neglect or infraction is regularly met, in threat or in fact, by the application of physical force by an individual or group possessing the socially recognized privilege of so acting.
   - The setting is usually very rigid and formalized (i.e., formalized courtroom setting).

2. Processual: focuses on the dispute-settlement process, rather than the rule itself.
   - Under the processual analysis, law is defined by its function (and not its form). Does the decision function to settle a dispute? Here you must look at social arrangements, sociological realities, cultural mechanisms, which act toward the enforcement of law.

   - Law: rules or modes of conduct made obligatory by some sanction, which is imposed and enforced for their violation by a controlling authority.

Mechanisms of Dispute Resolution

- Interpersonal violence: eye for an eye, a tooth for a tooth.
- Channeling conflict into ritual. Example: sports or ritual dances.
- Shaming. Example: public harangue.
- Supernatural agencies and ostracism. Example: the use of witchcraft and sorcery.
- Talking. Examples: bilateral negotiation, mediation, and umpires (arbitrator and adjudicator).

4. War

- Forms of war include:
  1. Raiding

2. Feuding
3. Warfare

Raiding

- A short-term use of force with a limited goal (stealing females, cattle, material goods). Example: the Achuar who live in the Amazonian border region of Ecuador and Peru (Descola 1996 [1993], 1994 [1986]).

Feuding

- Chronic hostilities between groups, neighbors, or kin. Example: the Dani case (Heider 1970). Nuer blood feuds and revenge (Evans-Pritchard 1940).

Warfare

- Violent conflicts involving communities, ethnic groups, and political units. The final objective is the domination of one society over the other.

Explanations of Warfare

- Ecological motivation
- Competition
- Evolutionary explanation

Ecological Motivation

- Limitation of resources
- Animal depletion or protein scarcity
- Scarcity of raw materials

Competition

- Social
- Economic
- Ideological

Evolutionary Explanation

- Male competition to increase differential reproductive success. Example: the Yanomamö and the study of Napoleon Chagnon (1983).

Forms of Resistance to Political and Social Domination

Physical Resistance

- Sabotage
- Guerrilla activity
- Rebellions or revolts

Moral Resistance

- Other forms of warfare
- Shamanic warfare

CHAPTER TWENTY-SEVEN

Cultures and Imagined Communities

Beyond the Direct Links of the Individual to the Social Group

- We now have to go beyond small-scale interactions of the individual with the social group.
- The most fundamental link is with the family or nuclear family unit.
- The next levels are the kinship networks.
- These can have short time depth and spatial location (i.e., nuclear family, extended family), or they can have longer time depth and involve more spatial dispersion (i.e., clan, moiety, lineage).
- All involve concepts of distinction between "us" and "them."

- We now move into the realm of identifying larger scale groups involving more people, larger territories, and in some cases, longer time depths.
- Again, these group definitions are all based on the individual's perception of the group she/he belong to or are assigned to.
- Defined in terms of "us" and "them."
- Choice of group affiliation to the individual is a means of assuring or attempting to assure reproductive success and the success and survival of children.

Imagined Communities

- The following definitions are derived from Maybury-Lewis (2002).

- These next levels of social classification are often termed "imagined communities," as their constitution or make-up changes with external and internal forces and the perception of the individual.
- Early works on these concepts can be found in Anderson (1983) and Barth (1969).

- Culture: a term that indicates the totality of ideas, attitudes, customs, and ways of doing things that people acquire as members of a society.
- Culture is also an imagined concept utilized to describe a people's or group's way of life.

- These "imagined communities" or social entities include:
- Indigenous groups
- Ethnic groups
- States
- Nation

Indigenous Groups

- Indigenous peoples: those that claim lands, because they were there first or have occupied them since time immemorial.
- Again, we see both a spatial aspect (extent of territory under control) and a temporal aspect (first people in time to occupy the territory).

- Tribal peoples: an imprecise term used today to refer to small-scale, pre-industrial societies that live in comparative isolation and manage their affairs without any centralized authority, such as a state.
- Indigenous and tribal peoples are generally underprivileged minorities within states that may face the threat of genocide or ethnocide.
- Genocide: the physical extermination of a defined category of people. Example: the genocide of Jews by the Nazis during World War II.
- Ethnocide: the destruction of a people's way of life. Example: the ethnocide of Native American cultures in North America from the eighteenth through the twentieth centuries.
- Another example of ethnocide: indigenismo—a policy developed in Mexico by President Benito Juárez in 1856. The policy was based on respect for the Indians while, at the same time, intending to assimilate them into the Mexican mainstream.

Ethnic Groups

- Ethnicity is like kinship in that people feel like kin through common descent but cannot trace the precise relationship.
- Ethnicity: group identity based on its members' ideas of their own distinctiveness from others. Based on a sense of common history linked to a particular area or territory.
- The terms ethnic groups and ethnicity are recent in origin, with use beginning in the 1950s as a means to identify sub-state groups that were in conflict throughout the world and who felt bound together by ties that lay between kinship and nationality.
- Again we see the basic themes of spatial territory based on a temporal link to shared ancestors and the formation of large group categories as a means of differentiating between "us" and "them."
- Such notions can be seen as mechanisms of survival based on the theory that more security is found in larger numbers of people/animals.
- Ethnicity is thus activated when human beings are under stress.
- Ethnic cleansing: the practice of massacring people of a different ethnic group in order to clear their territory for settlement by the attackers. Example: ethnic cleansing in the former Yugoslavia between the Croatians and Serbians in the 1980s and 1990s.

States

- State: a single, supreme authority over a group of people occupying a common territory (broad definition beginning in the seventeenth century).
- Another defining characteristic of the state is that it has a monopoly over the legitimate use of physical force.
- Based on the concept of society as a social contract, which all individuals enter into of their own free will (i.e., democracies)(see Weber 1930 [1904-1905, 1920]; Rousseau 1987 [1762]).

- Again notions of spatial territoriality are of extreme importance.
- Notion of individual free choice and equality are fundamental for the acceptance of the "state."
- Civil society: a term used to refer to those formal and informal ways that people generate themselves of coming together and communicating with each other.
- Link to temporal claims of ownership are often sought in the archaeological record (i.e., in historical archaeology or in the elimination of past histories or the archaeology of other groups).

Nations

- Nation: unit created by feelings of nationalism.
- Nationalism: the notion, emotion, or belief of a group occupying a particular territory that the nation and state should coincide; the desire of individuals with common historical roots to control a particular territory. This territory may or may not be defined and recognized externally as a state. However, the ultimate goal of the group (often ethnic group) is to have it recognized as such. Example: Kurds in Turkey and Iraq wanting their own state based on shared notions of ethnicity and nationalism.
- Nation-state: when the state corresponds to a single nation. Example: the United States of America.
- Nation-building: motivation of citizens to feel a sense of commitment to the state, rather than simply to their own people within the state.

Other Considerations

- All of these imagined communities change their boundaries through time.
- Individuals choose to belong to different groups at different times, helping to cause these boundaries to fluctuate through time.
- Symbols, as expressed in dress, food, behavior, language, etc., are utilized by individuals to reaffirm group memberships.
- Group memberships are often multiple and overlapping.

- Basic premise of the state is the protection of individual rights. This guarantee of individual protection and rights is the key to the legitimization or acceptance of the state by the individual.

- David Maybury-Lewis (2002, 128) brings up a good point when he discusses suggestions "that the state in multiethnic societies would have to defend collective as well as individual rights and, in effect, guarantee the circumstances under which ethnic groups can thrive." He rightly counters this by stating, "The problem with such a guarantee is, as we have seen, that it involves the state in the business of protecting group rights rather than the individual rights that have been at the heart of enlightenment thinking about democracy and the social contract."

CHAPTER TWENTY-EIGHT

Globalization and Resistance

Globalization from Above

- Globalization is about a world of things in motion. Examples: objects, persons, images, and discourses.
- Globalization can be seen as a means of crossing state and nation boundaries by circumventing those physical boundaries.
- It is an attempt to "open up" borders.
- Examples of ideas, people, etc. that can circumvent these boundaries include mass communication (the media), epidemics, tourism, and terrorism. All have the ability to cross the traditional physical boundaries or borders of states in non-traditional ways in common.

Potential Reasons

- Globalization can be understood as a particular contemporary configuration in the relationship between capital and nation-states.
- Global capital: characterized by strategies of predatory mobility (across both time and space).
- These predatory strategies can be seen as being geared toward acquiring wealth from individuals and resources from states and nations.
- Often, symbolism will be utilized to stress the necessity of acquiring particular goods, becoming a "member" of a particular group, or show the benefits of such market interactions.

Potential Problems or Worries

- Globalization is envisioned as a runaway horse without a rider (from William Grieder in 1997).
- Globalization is demonstrably creating increases in inequalities both within and across societies and creates a spiraling process of ecological degradation. It also creates unviable relationships between finance and manufacturing capital, as well as between goods and the wealth required to purchase them.
  1. Markets and deregulation produce a concentration of wealth and increases in inequality.
  2. Collapse of nation-states (a world without borders).
  3. Favors corporativism. The creation of multi-national corporations, which control the world's wealth and have few regulations
- People are afraid of global agencies (for example, global banks). We do not know what the global agencies are up to. Examples: World Trade Organization, The North American Free Trade Agreement, United Nations.
- This leads to the characterization that with globalization, information, resources, money, etc., move from above or from larger non-local entities like multinational corporations or federal governments to below or to more local and smaller entities like villages, towns, other communities, kinship groups, families, etc.

Potential Benefits

- The idea of progress: the development of an individual or society in a direction considered more beneficial than and superior to the previous level:
  1. Sequence toward perfection.
  2. Lineal: one way ticket to development. Today this is seen in concepts of sustainable development.
  3. Directional: having a final objective. Free markets and liberal democracy.
- Successful examples: democratization of the world such as possibly in areas of the Middle East like Iraq, though this processes is obviously still occurring and the outcomes are not completely known; the triumph of capitalism, with examples including the economic miracles of Taiwan, Hong Kong, Singapore, Korea, Chile, and Turkey.

Globalization from Below: A Few Examples

- Example 1. The formation of cooperatives to sustain ethnic diversity and to take advantage of economic niches that involve the production and distribution of local products to the world market.
- Cooperatives can be seen as economic structures whereby individuals of similar backgrounds, ethnicity, etc. group together to contend with larger-scale economic forces beyond their control.
- This can be seen as a more resilient or adaptive strategy than what the individual could hope to accomplish or obtain on her/his own.

- Example 2. The development and use of non-governmental organizations (NGOs).
- Objective: Equity, access, justice, and redistribution.
- Arena of actions:
    1. Official public sphere
    2. International civil societies' initiatives
    3. Local communities

- Origins of NGOs, also known as transnational advocacy networks:
- Labor
- Suffrage
- Civil rights
- Environmentalism

- NGOs and nation-states:
- Opposition to or complaints about policies
- Politicize force
- Favors transparency

The Conflicts

- Globalization and cultural diversity: questions include whether a global similar culture is beneficial or progressive or perhaps is not such a good idea wherefore the preservation of diversity including cultural diversity is more beneficial to sustain the growing global population.

- Indigenous peoples' populations. Loss of identity.
- Agricultural diversity. Loss of diversity.
- Gene pirates. Stealing of information, both intellectual and biological.
- Patent power and gene banks. Limiting control of access to important resources.
- Genetically manipulated foods. Changing the genetic structure of important resources.

Problems versus Progress

- Deforestation. New and continued supply of products.
- Loss of indigenous territories. Transmigration, new land for peoples from overpopulated areas.
- Local need for money and jobs. Free trade and access to industrialized goods.
- Cash crops and loss of diversity. Increase production of crops in world demand.
- Loss of local cultural practices. One culture/language and media access.
- Debt. Profit/wealth to producers.

Getting Beyond Cultural Relativism to the Individual

- The Universal Declaration of Human Rights (adopted by the United Nations on December 10 of 1948)(http://www.un.org/en/documents/udhr/history.shtml).
- Legal treaties: civil, political, economic, cultural.
- International Covenant on Civil and Political Rights (adopted by the United Nations on December 16 of 1966)(http://legal.un.org/avl/ha/iccpr/iccpr.html)

- Cases:
- Capital punishment of minors and abortion
- Free marriage choice. Egyptian rights to divorce.
- Freedom of religion
- United Nations Security Council and racism

Problem: How to balance the rights of the individual, the rights of society, and the common good

- Possible solutions:
- The right to choose
- The right to exit a group
- Movement toward a universal jurisdiction and international criminal court: war crimes and crimes against humanity
- Universal education

Bibliography

Aikio, Pekka. 1989. "The Changing Role of Reindeer in the Life of the Sámi." In *The Walking Larder. Patterns of Domestication, Pastoralism, and Predation*, edited by J. Clutton-Brock, 169-184. London: Unwin Hyman, One World Archaeology.

Allen, John L. and Audrey C. Shalinsky. 2004. *Student Atlas of Anthropology*. New York: McGraw-Hill Publishers.

Anderson, Benedict. 1983. *Imagined Communities: Reflections on the Origin and Spread of Nationalism*. London: Verso.

Anderson, Stephen R. 2010.   *How Many Languages Are There in the World?* Brochure Series: Frequently Asked Questions. Linguistic Society of America, Washington, D.C.

Barth, Fredrik. 1969.   *Ethnic Groups and Boundaries*. Boston: Little Brown.

Bellwood, Peter. 2013. *First Migrants: Ancient Migration in Global Perspective*. Malden, MA: Wiley, Blackwell.

Bellwood, Peter. 2005. *First Farmers: The Origins of Agricultural Societies*. Malden, MA: Blackwell.

Benedict, Ruth Fulton. 1954 [1946].   *The Chrysanthemum and the Sword: Patterns of Japanese Culture*. Vermont: C. E. Tuttle, Rutland.

Benedict, Ruth Fulton. 1934. *Patterns of Culture*. New York: Houghton Mifflin Company.

Berger, Lee R., Hawks, John, De Ruiter, Darryl J., Churchill, Steven E., Schmid, Peter, Delezene, Lucas K., Kivell, Tracy L., Garvin, Heather M., Williams, Scott A., Desilva, Jeremy M., Skinner, Matthew M., Musiba, Charles M., Cameron, Noel, Holliday, Trenton W., Harcourt - Smith, William, Ackermann, Rebecca R., Bastir, Markus, Bogin, Barry, Bolter, Debra, Brophy, Juliet, Cofran, Zachary D., Congdon, Kimberly A., Deane, Andrew S., Dembo, Mana, Drapeau, Michelle, Elliott, Marina C., Feuerriegel, Elen M., Garcia - Martinez, Daniel, Green, David J., Gurtov, Alia, Irish, Joel D., Kruger, Ashley, Laird, Myra F., Marchi, Damiano, Meyer, Marc R., Nalla, Shahed, Negash,

Enquye W., Orr, Caley M., Radovcic, Davorka, Schroeder, Lauren, Scott, Jill E., Throckmorton, Zachary, Tocheri, Matthew W., Vansickle, Caroline, Walker, Christopher S., Wei, Pianpian, Zipfel, Bernhard. 2015. Homo naledi, a New Species of the Genus Homo from Dinaledi Chamber, South Africa. *ELIFE*, 4: e09560.

Beukens, R. P., L.A. Pavlish, R.G.V. Hancock, R.M. Farquhar, G.C. Wilson, P.J. Julig, and William Ross. 1992. "Radiocarbon Dating of Copper Preserved Organics." *Radiocarbon* 34 (3): 890–897.

Binford, Lewis R. 2001. *Constructing Frames of Reference: An Analytical Method for Archaeological Theory Building Using Ethnographic and Environmental Data*. Berkeley: University of California Press.

Binford, Lewis R. 1989. *Debating Archaeology*. San Diego: Academic Press.

Binford, Lewis R. 1988. *In Pursuit of the Past: Decoding the Archaeological Record*. New York: Thames and Hudson.

Binford, Lewis R. 1984. *Faunal Remains from Klasies River Mouth*. New York: Academic Press, Inc.

Boada Rivas, Ana Maria. 1987. *Asentamientos Indigenas en el Valle de La Laguna (Samacá – Boyacá)*. Fundación de Investigaciones Arqueológicas Nacionales. No. 35. Banco de la República, Bogotá.

Boas, Franz. 1940. *Race, Language, and Culture*. New York: The Macmillan Company.

Boaz, Franz. 1938 [1911]. *The Mind of Primitive Man*. Revised edition. New York: The Macmillan Company.

Bonzani, Renée M., George M. Crothers, Patrick Trader, Robert H. Ward, and Ronald R. Switzer. 2007.

"Early Sunflower Head Remains from Mammoth Cave, Kentucky, U.S.A." *Journal of Ethnobiology* 27(1):73-87.

Bonzani, Renée M. and Augusto Oyuela-Caycedo. 2006. "The Gift of the Variation and Dispersion of Maize: Social and Technological Context in Amerindian Societies." In *Histories of Maize: Multidisciplinary Approaches to the Prehistory, Biogeography, Domestication, and Evolution of Maize,* edited by John Staller, Robert Tykot, and Bruce Benz, 343-356. New York: Elsevier/ Academic Press.

Boserup, Ester. 1965. *The Conditions of Agricultural Growth: The Economics of Agrarian Change Under Population Pressure*. New York: Aldine Publishing Company.

Bourdieu, Pierre. 1977. *Outline of a Theory of Practice*. Cambridge Studies in Social and Cultural Anthropology. Cambridge, UK: Cambridge University Press.

Boyd, Robert and Joan B. Silk. 2015. *How Humans Evolved*. Seventh edition. New York: W. W. Norton and Company.

Boyd, Robert and Joan B. Silk. 2000. *How Humans Evolved*. Second edition. New York: W. W. Norton and Company.

Braudel, Fernand. 1981 [1979]. *The Structures of Everyday Life: Civilization & Capitalism 15th - 18th Century.* Volume 1. New York: Harper & Row, Publishers.

Browman, David L. and Steven Williams. 2002. *New Perspectives on the Origins of Americanist Archaeology.* Tuscaloosa: University of Alabama Press.

Cabrera, G., C. Franky, and D. Mahecha. 1999. *Los Nukak: Nómadas de la Amazonía Colombíana.* Bogotá: Editorial Universidad Nacional,

Carmichael, Patrick H. 1995. "Nasca Burial Patterns: Social Structure and Mortuary Ideology." In *Tombs for the Living: Andean Mortuary Practices,* edited by Tom D. Dillehay. Washington, D.C.: Dumbarton Oaks Research Library and Collection.

Carter, Howard. 1972. *The Tomb of Tutankhamen.* New York: E. P. Dutton & Co., Inc.

Cashdan, Elizabeth. 1990. *Risk and Uncertainty in Tribal and Peasant Economies.* Boulder, CO: Westview Press.

Cavalli-Sforza, Luigi Lucas and Francesco Cavalli-Sforza. 1996. *The Great Human Diaspora: The History of Diversity and Evolution.* Cambridge, MA: Perseus Publishing.

Chagnon, Napoleon A. 1983. *Yanomamö: The Fierce People.* Third edition. New York: Holt, Rinehart, and Winston.

Chomsky, Noam. 1981. *Lectures on Government and Binding: The Pisa Lectures.* Holland: Foris, Dordrecht.

Chomsky, Noam. 1965. *Aspects of the Theory of Syntax.* Cambridge, MA: MIT Press.

Chomsky, Noam. 1957. *Syntactic Structures.* The Hague, Netherlands: Mouton.

Clark, J. E. and M. Blake. 1994. "The Power of Prestige: Competitive Generosity and the Emergence of Rank in Lowland Mesoamerica." In *Factional Competition and Political Development in the New World,* edited by E. M. Brumfiel and J. W. Fox, 17-30. Cambridge, UK: Cambridge University Press.

Clutton-Brock, J., ed. 1989. *The Walking Larder: Patterns of Domestication, Pastoralism, and Predation.* London: Unwin Hyman.

Coe, Michael D. and Rex Koontz. 2002. *Mexico: From the Olmecs to the Aztecs.* New York: Thames and Hudson.

Cooper, Frederick and Ann Stoler, eds. 1997. *Tensions of Empire: Colonial Cultures in a Bourgeois World.* Berkeley: University of California Press.

Darwin, Charles. 1859. *On the Origin of Species by Means of Natural Selection, or the Preservation of Favoured Races in the Struggle for Life.* London: John Murray.

Descola, Phillipe. 1994 [1986]. *In the Society of Nature: A native ecology in Amazonia,* Translated from the French by Nora Scott. Cambridge, UK: Cambridge University Press.

Descola, Philippe. 1996 [1993]. *The Spears of Twilight: Life and Death in the Amazon Jungle,.* Translated from the French by Janet Lloyd. London: Harper Collins Publishers.

"Declaration of Independence," The Charters of Freedom, accessed June 10, 2015, http://www.archives.gov/exhibits/charters/declaration_transcript.html

Dick, Herbert W. 1965. *Bat Cave*. The School of American Research. Monograph No. 27. Santa Fe, New Mexico.

Doran, Glen H., ed. 2002. *Windover: Multidisciplinary Investigations of an Early Archaic Florida Cemetery*. Gainesville, FL: University of Florida Press.

Douglas, Mary. 1970. *Purity and Danger: An Analysis of Concepts of Pollution and Taboo*. London: Routledge & Kegan Paul.

"Drawing From the Past: Maya Antiquity Through the Eyes of Frederick Catherwood," Smith College, accessed June 9, 2015, http://www.smith.edu/libraries/libs/rarebook/exhibitions/catherwood/index.htm

Driver, Harold E. 1961. *Indians of North America*. Chicago: University of Chicago Press.

Duane, O. B. 1996. *Celtic Art*. London: Brockhampton Press.

Durkheim, Emile. 2001 [1912]. *Elementary Forms of Religious Life*. Translated by Carol Cosman. New York: Oxford University Press.

Durkheim, Emile. 1947 [1893]. *The Division of Labor in Society*. Glencoe, IL: Free Press.

Eliade, Mircea. 1978. *The Forbidden Forest*. Notre Dame: University of Notre Dame Press.

Eliade, Mircea. 1952. *Images et Symboles: Essais sur Symbolisme Magico-Religieux*. Paris: Gallimard.

"Ethics Resources," American Anthropological Association, accessed June 9, 2015, http://www.aaanet.org/cmtes/ethics/Ethics-Resources.cfm

Evans-Pritchard, Edward Evan. 1940. *The Nuer, a Description of the Modes of Livelihood and Political Institutions of a Nilotic people*. Oxford: Clarendon Press.

Everett, Daniel L. 2008. *Don't Sleep: There Are Snakes. Life and Language in the Amazonian Jungle*. New York: Random House, Inc.

"Explore the Form," United States 2010 Census, accessed June 9, 2015, http://www.census.gov/2010census/about/interactive-form.php

Finegan, Edward. 2015. *Language: Its Structure and Use*. Seventh edition. Stamford, CT: Cengage Learning.

Flannery, Kent, ed. 1986. *Guila Naquitz: Archaic Foraging and Early Agriculture in Oaxaca, Mexico*. Orlando: Academic Press.

Flannery, Kent. 1973. The Origins of Agriculture. *Annual Review of Anthropology* (2): 271–310.

Ford, Richard. 1985. "The Processes of Plant Food Production in Prehistoric North America." In *Prehistoric Food Production in North America*, edited by Richard I. Ford, 1- 18. Anthropological Papers No. 75. Museum of Anthropology, University of Michigan, Ann Arbor.

Fox, Robin. 1967. *Kinship and Marriage*. Baltimore: Penguin Books.

Frazer, James G. 1911–1915 [1890] *The Golden Bough: A Study in Magic and Religion*. Third edition. London: The Macmillan Company.

Frazer, James G. 1910. *Totemism and Exogamy, a Treatise on Certain Early Forms of Superstition and Society*. London: The Macmillan Company.

Frost, Peter. 2014. "The Puzzle of European Hair, Eye, and Skin Color." *Advances in Anthropology* (4): 78-88. Published Online May 2014 in SciRes. http://www.scirp.org/journal/aa http://dx.doi.org/10.4236/aa.2014.42011

Gallagher, James P. and Constance M. Arzigian. 1994. "A New Perspective on Late Prehistoric Agricultural Intensification in the Upper Mississippi River Valley." In *Agricultural Origins and Development in the Midcontinent*, Report 19, edited by William Green, 171-188. Iowa City: University of Iowa Press.

Geertz, Clifford. 1973. *The Interpretation of Cultures*. New York: Basic Book.

Geertz, Clifford. 1963 *Peddlers and Princes: Social Change and Economic Modernization in Two Indonesian*. Chicago: University of Chicago Press.

Gibbons, Ann. 2009. "A New Kind of Ancestor: *Ardipithecus* Unveiled." *Science 326*: 36–40.

Gillispie, Charles Coulston and Michel Dewachter, eds. 1987. *Monuments of Egypt. The Napoleonic Edition. The Complete Archaeological Plates from La Description de L'Egypte*. Princeton, NJ: Princeton Architectural Press.

Goodenough, W. 1951. *Property, Kin, and Community on Truk*. New Haven, CT: Yale University.

Grant, Michael. 1979. *The Art and Life of Pompeii and Herculaneum*. New York: Newsweek.

Grieder, William. 1997. *One World, Ready or Not: The Manic Logic of Global Capitalism*. New York: Simon and Schuster.

Hames, Raymond. 1990. "Sharing Among the Yanomamö: Part I, The Effects of Risk." In *Risk and Uncertainty in Tribal and Peasant Economies*, edited by Elizabeth Cashdan, 89-106. Boulder, CO: Westview Press.

Hames, Raymond and William Vickers. 1983. *Adaptive Responses of Native Amazonians*. New York: Academic Press.

Harris, Marvin 1989 [1974]. *Cows, Pigs, Wars, & Witches: The Riddles of Culture*. New York: Vintage Books.

Harris, Marvin. 1979. *Cultural Materialism: The Struggle for a Science of Culture*. Updated edition (2001). Walnut Creek, CA: AltaMira Press.

Harris, Marvin. 1968. *Rise of Anthropological Theory: A History of Theories of Culture*. New York: Crowell.

Heider, Karl G. 1970. *The Dugum Dani: A Papuan Culture in the Highlands of West New Guinea*. Viking Fund Publications in Anthropology Number Forty-Nine. New York, New York: Wenner-Gren Foundation for Anthropological Research.

Herskovitz, Melville J. 1952. *Economic Anthropology: A Study in Comparative Economics*. New York: A. A. Knopf.

Herskovitz. 1940. *The Economic Life of Primitive Peoples*. New York: A. A. Knopf.

Hodder, Ian, ed. 2002. *Archaeological Theory Today*. Second edition. Cambridge, MA: Polity Press.

Hodder, Ian. 1986. *Reading the Past: Current Approaches to Interpretation in Archaeology*. New York: Cambridge University Press.

Hodder, Ian, ed. 1982. *Symbolic and Structural Archaeology*. New York: Cambridge University Press.

"Human Relation Area Files," Yale University, accessed June 9, 2015, http://hraf.yale.edu/

"International Covenant on Civil and Political Rights," United Nations, Audiovisual Library of International Law, accessed June 10, 2015, http://legal.un.org/avl/ha/iccpr/iccpr.html

Johanson, Donald and Maitland Edey. 1981. *Lucy. The Beginnings of Humankind*. New York: Simon and Schuster.

Keeton, William T. 1976. *Biological Sciences*. Third edition. New York: W. W. Norton & Company.

Kelly, Raymond C. 1976. "Witchcraft and Sexual Relations: An Exploration in the Social and Semantic Implications of the Structure of Belief." In *Man and Woman in the New Guinea Highlands*, edited by P. Brown and G. Buchbinder, 36-53. Special Publication, no. 8. American Anthropological Association, Washington, D.C.

"Kinship Symbols," University of Wisconsin, Green Bay, accessed June 10, 2015, http://www.uwgb.edu/walterl/kinship/304Symbols.htm

Klineberg, O. 1951. "Race and Psychology." In *The Race Question in Modern Science*. UNESCO, Paris.

Kottak, Conrad Phillip. 2013. *Anthropology: Appreciating Human Diversity*. Fifteenth edition. New York: McGraw-Hill.

Kottak, Conrad Phillip and Kathryn A. Kozaitis. 2003. *On Being Different. Diversity and Multiculturalism in the North American Mainstream*. Second edition. New York: McGraw-Hill.

Kroeber, Alfred L. 1944. *Configurations of Cultural Growth*. Berkeley: University of California Press.

Leach, Edmund. 1954. *Political Systems of Highland Burm: A Study of Kachin Social Structure*. Cambridge, MA: Harvard University Press.

Lee, Richard B. 1979. *The !Kung San: Men, Women and Work in a Foraging Society*. Cambridge, New York: Cambridge University Press.

Lévi-Strauss, Claude. 1969. *The Elementary Structures of Kinship (Les structures élémentaires de la parenté)*. Revised ed. translated from the French by James Harle Bell, John Richard von Sturmer, and Rodney Needham, editor. London: Eyre & Spottiswoode.

Lévi-Strauss, Claude. 1969. *The Raw and the Cooked*. Translated from the French by John and Doreen Weightman. New York: Harper and Row.

Lévi-Strauss, Claude. 1967. *Structural Anthropology*. New York: Basic Books.

Lévi-Strauss, Claude. 1966. *The Savage Mind (Pensée Sauvage)*. Chicago: University of Chicago Press.

Lewis, Oscar. 1966. *La Vida: A Puerto Rican Family in the Culture of Poverty – San Juan and New York*. New York: Random House.

Lewis, Oscar. 1959. *Five Families: Mexican Case Studies in the Culture of Poverty*. New York: Basic Books.

Linton, Ralph. 1955. *The Tree of Culture*. New York: Knopf.

Linton, Ralph. 1936. *The Study of Man*. New York: D. Appleton-Century Company, Incorporated.

Lubbock, John, Sir. 1889. *The Origins of Civilization and the Primitive Condition of Man: Mental and Social Condition of Savages*. New York: Appleton.

Lubbock, John, Sir. 1865. *Prehistoric Times as Illustrated by Ancient Remains, and the Manners and Customs of Modern Savages*. London: Williams and Norgate.

Lyell, Charles, Sir. 1841 [1833]. *Elements of Geology*. Reprinted from the second English edition from the original plates and woodcuts, under the direction of the author. Boston: Hilliard, Gray.

Lyon, Danny. 1992. *Memories of the Southern Civil Rights Movement*. Series: Lyndhurst Series on the South. Published for the Center for Documentary Studies, Duke University, by University of North Carolina Press, Chapel Hill, North Carolina.

Lyotard, Jean François. 1993. *The Postmodern Explained*. Minneapolis: University of Minnesota Press.

Maine, Sir Henry Sumner. 1960 [1861]. *Ancient Law: Its Connection With the Early History of Society, and Its Relations to Modern Ideas*. Revised edition. New York: Button; London and Toronto: Dent.

Malinowski, Bronislaw. 1944. *A Scientific Theory of Culture*. Chapel Hill, NC: University of North Carolina Press.

Malinowski, Bronislaw. 1922. *Argonauts of the Western Pacific: an Account of Native Enterprise and Adventure in the Archipelagoes of Melanesian New Guinea*. New York: E.P. Dutton & Co; London: G. Routledge & Sons, Ltd.

Mangelsdorf, Paul C. 1974. *Corn: Its Origins, Evolution, and Improvement*. Cambridge, MA: The Belknap Press of Harvard University Press.

Mangelsdorf, Paul C., H. W. Dick, and J. Cámara-Hernández. 1967. "Bat Cave Revisited." *Botanical Museum Leaflet Harvard University* 22: 1–31.

Marcus, George and Michael Fischer. 1986. *Anthropology as Cultural Critique: An Experimental Moment in the Human Sciences*. Chicago: University of Chicago Press.

Marcus, Joyce and Kent Flannery. 1996. *Zapotec Civilization: How Urban Society Evolved in Mexico's Oaxaca*. New York: Thames and Hudson, New York.

Marx, Karl. 1867. *Capital*. Chicago: Charles H. Kerr and Co.

Marx, Karl and Friedrich Engels. 1848. *Manifest der kommunistischen Partei*. London: The Communist League.

Mauss, Marcel. 1966 [1925]. *The Gift: Forms and Functions of Exchange in Archaic Societies*. London: Cohen & West, Ltd.

Maybury-Lewis, David. 2002. *Indigenous Peoples, Ethnic Groups, and the State*. Second edition. Cultural Studies in Ethnicity and Change. Boston: Allyn and Bacon.

Mead, Margaret. 1949 [1928]. *Coming of Age in Samoa*. New York: Mentor Books.

Mead, Margaret. 1935. *Sex and Temperament in Three Primitive Societies*. New York: W. Morrow & company.

Mendel, Gregor. 1870 [1866] *Versuche Über Pflanzenhybriden*. Ostwald's Klassiker der Exakten Wissenschaften. Nr. 121. Zwei Abhandlungen. Wulhelm Englelmann in Leipzig.

Mintz, Sidney. 1985. *Sweetness and Power: The Place of Sugar in Modern History*. New York: Penguin Books.

Morgan, Lewis Henry. 1877. *Ancient Society; or, Researches in the Lines of Human Progress from Savagery, through Barbarism to Civilization*. New York: H. Holt and Company.

Morgan, Lewis Henry. 1871. *Systems of Consanguinity and Affinity of the Human Family*. Washington, D.C.: Smithsonian Institution.

Morgan, Lewis Henry. 1904 [1851]. *League of the Ho-dé-no-sau-nee or Iroquois*. Revised edition. New York: Dodd, Mead.

Nadel, Dani, Dolores R. Piperno, Irene Holst, Ainit Snir, and Ehud Weiss. 2012. "New Evidence for the processing of wild cereal grains at Ohalo II, a 23,000-year-old campsite on the shore of the Sea of Galilee, Israel." *Antiquity* 86: 990–1003.

Nolan, Patrick and Gerhard Lenski. 2006. *Human Societies: An Introduction to Macrosociology*. Tenth edition. Boulder, CO: Paradigm Publishers.

Ortner, Sherry B. 1984. "Theory in Anthropology Since the Sixties." *Comparative Studies in Society and History* 26(1): 126–166.

Oyuela-Caycedo, Augusto and Renée M. Bonzani. 2014. *San Jacinto 1: Ecologia Historica, Origenes de la Ceramica, e Inicios de la Vida Sedentaria en el Caribe Colombiano*. Spanish edition. Colombia: Universidad del Norte.

Oyuela-Caycedo, Augusto and Renée M. Bonzani. 2005. *San Jacinto 1: A Historical Ecological Approach to an Archaic Site in Colombia*. Tuscaloosa: University of Alabama Press.

Pearsall, Deborah M. 2000. *Paleoethnobotany: A Handbook of Procedures*. Second edition. New York: Academic Press.

Pianka, Eric R. 1988. *Evolutionary Ecology*. New York: Harper & Row.

Polanyi, Karl. 1944. *The Great Transformation*. New York: Farrar & Rinehart, Inc.

"Press Kit. Stanford Blood Center Facts," Stanford School of Medicine, accessed June 9, 2015, http://bloodcenter.stanford.edu/press/press_kit.html

Price, T. Douglas. 2009. "Ancient Farming in Eastern North America." *Proceedings of the National Academy of Sciences* (PNAS) 106 (16): 6427–6428.

Price, T. Douglass and Gary M. Feinman. 2008. *Images of the Past*. Fifth edition. New York: McGraw-Hill.

Rabey, Mario A. 1986. "Are Llama-herders in the South Central Andes True Pastoralists?" In *The Walking Larder. Patterns of Domestication, Pastoralism, and Predation*, edited by J. Clutton-Brock, 267–276. One World Archaeology. London: Unwin Hyman.

Radcliffe-Brown, Alfred Reginald. 1952. *Structure and Function in Primitive Societies*. Glencoe, IL: Free Press.

Radcliffe-Brown, Alfred Reginald. 1933. *The Andaman Islanders*. Cambridge, UK: The University Press.

Rappaport, Roy. 1967. *Pigs for the Ancestors: Ritual in the Ecology of a New Guinea People*. New Haven, CT: Yale University Press.

Ratzel, Friedrich. 1896. *The History of Mankind*. New York: MacMillan and Co., Ltd.

Ratzel, Friedrich. 1894 [1885-1888]. *Völkerkunde. 2, gänzlich neub eard. aufl.* Leipzig: Wien, Bibliographisches Institut.

Reiter, Rayna R. ed. 1975. *Toward an Anthropology of Women*. New York: Monthly Review Press.

Renfrew, Colin and Paul Bahn. 2012. *Archaeology: Theories, Methods and Practice*. Sixth edition. New York: Thames & Hudson.

Renfrew, Colin and Paul Bahn. 2004. *Archaeology: Theories, Methods and Practice*. Fourth edition. New York: Thames & Hudson.

Renfrew, Colin and Paul Bahn. 2000. *Archaeology: Theories, Methods and Practice*. Third edition. New York: Thames & Hudson.

Roosevelt, A. C., R. A. Housley, M. Imazio da Silveira, S. Maranca, and R. Johnson. 1991. "Eighth Millennium Pottery from a Prehistoric Shell Midden in the Brazilian Amazon." *Science* 254: 1621–1624.

Rosaldo, Michelle and Louise Lamphere eds. 1974. *Women, Culture, and Society*. Stanford, CA: Stanford University Press.

Rosenthal, Theodore and Bernard J. Siegel. 1959. "Magic and Witchcraft: An Interpretation from Dissonance Theory." *Southwestern Journal of Anthropology* 15(2): 143-167.

Rousseau, Jean-Jacques. 1987 [1762]. *The Social Contract*. New York: Penguin Books.

Sahlins, Marshall David. 1972. *Stone Age Economics*. Chicago: Aldine-Atherton.

Sahlins, Marshall David. 1968. "Notes on the Original Affluent Society." In *Man the Hunter* edited by R.B. Lee and I. DeVore, 85–89. New York: Aldine Publishing Company.

Sapir, Edward. 1921. *Language: An Introduction to the Study of Speech.* New York: Harcourt, Brace, & World.

Schaan, Denise Pahl. 2008. "The Nonagricultural Chiefdoms of Marajó Island." In *Handbook of South American Archaeology,* edited by Helaine Silverman and William H. Isbell, 339–357. New York: Springer.

Schliemann, Heinrich. 1976 [1884]. *Troja. Results of the Latest Researches and Discoveries on the Site of Homer's Troy, 1882.* Reprinted Edition. New York: Arno Press.

Schliemann, Heinrich. 1976 [1881]. *Ilios: The City and Country of the Trojans.* Reprinted Edition. New York: Arno Press.

Schultes, Richard Evans and Albert Hofmann. 1992. *Plants of the Gods: Their Sacred, Healing and Hallucinogenic Powers.* Rochester, VT: Healing Arts Press.

Schultes, Richard Evans and Robert F. Raffauf. 1990. *The Healing Forest: Medicinal and Toxic Plants of the Northwest Amazonia.* Portland, OR: Dioscorides Press.

Sharma, A. and A. Gupta, eds. 2006. *The Anthropology of the State: A Reader.* Malden, MA: Blackwell.

Siegel, James. 2006. *Naming the Witch.* Stanford, CA: Stanford University Press.

Smith, Adam. 1776. *An Inquiry into the Nature and Causes of the Wealth of Nations.* London: W. Strahan and T. Cadell.

Smith, Bruce D. 2014. "The Domestication of *Helianthus annuus* L. (Sunflower)." *Veget Hist Archaeobot.* 23:57–74.

Smith, Bruce D. 2011. "The Cultural Context of Plant Domestication in Eastern North America." *Current Anthropology.* 52(S4): S471–S484.

Smith, Bruce D. 2006. "Eastern North America as an Independent Center of Plant Domestication." *Proceedings of the National Academy of Sciences (PNAS).* 10333: 12223–12228.

Smith, Bruce D. 1998. *The Emergence of Agriculture.* New York: Scientific American Library.

Smith, Bruce D. 1992. *Rivers of Change: Essays on Early Agriculture in Eastern North America.* Washington, D.C.: Smithsonian Institution Press.

Smith, Bruce D. 1987. "Independent Domestication of Indigenous Seed-Bearing Plants in Eastern North America." In *Emergent Horticultural Economies of the Eastern Woodlands,* edited by W. F. Keegan, 3–47. Occasional Paper No. 7. Carbondale: Center for Archaeological Investigations, Southern Illinois University.

Smith, Bruce D. 1984. "*Chenopodium* as a Prehistoric Domesticate in Eastern North America: Evidence from Russell Cave, Alabama." *Science.* 226: 165–168.

Smith, Bruce D. and C. W. Cowan. 2003. "Domesticated Crop Plants and the Evolution of Food Production Economies in Eastern North America." In *People and Plants in Ancient Eastern North America,* edited by P. E. Minnis, 105–125. Washington, D.C.: Smithsonian Books.

Smith, Bruce D. and Richard A. Yarnell. 2009. "Initial Formation of an Indigenous Crop Complex in Eastern North America at 3800 BP." *Proceedings of the National Academy of Sciences* (PNAS) 106(16): 6561–6566.

Staller, John, Robert Tykot, and Bruce Benz. 2006. *Histories of Maize: Multidisciplinary Approaches to the Prehistory, Biogeography, Domestication, and Evolution of Maize.* New York: Elsevier/ Academic Press, New York.

Stein, Philip L. and Bruce M. Rowe. 2000. *Physical Anthropology.* Seventh edition. New York: McGraw-Hill.

Stephens, John Lloyd. 1973 [1845]. *Incidents of Travel in Yucatán. Volumes I and II.* With Engravings by Frederick Catherwood. Edited and with an introductin by Victor Wolfgang von Hagen. Norman, OK: University of Oklahoma Press.

Steward, Julian H. 1963. *Handbook of South American Indians.* 7 volumes. Smithsonian Institution. New York: Cooper Square Publishers.

Steward, Julian H. 1955. *Theory of Culture Change: The Methodology of Multilinear Evolution.* Urbana, IL: University of Illinois Press.

Stoler, Ann. 2002. *Carnal Knowledge and Imperial Power: Race and the Intimate in Colonial Rule.* Berkeley: University of California Press.

Strickberger, Monroe W. 1990. *Evolution.* Boston: Jones and Bartlett Publishers.

Stuart, Gene S. 1981. *The Mighty Aztec.* Photographs by Mark Godfrey. Special Publications Division National Geographic Society, Washington, D.C.

Sugiyama, Saburo. 2005. *Human Sacrifice, Militarism, and Rulership: Materialization of State Ideology at the Feathered Serpent Pyramid, Teotihuacan.* New York: Cambridge University Press.

"The Universal Declaration of Human Rights," United Nations, accessed June 10, 2015, http:// www.un.org/en/documents/udhr/history.shtml

Thomsen, C. J. 1848 [1836]. *Ledetraad til Nordisk Oldkundskab* (Guide to Northern Antiquity). Selskabet.

Trigger, Bruce. 2006. *A History of Archaeological Thought.* Second edition. Oxford: Cambridge University Press.

Turner, Victor. 1982. *From Ritual to Theatre: The Human Seriousness of Play.* New York: Performing Arts Journal Publications.

Turner, Victor. 1974. *Dramas, Fields, and Metaphors: Symbolic Action in Humans.* Ithaca, NY: Cornell University Press.

Turner, Victor. 1967. *The Forest of Symbols: Aspects of Ndembu Ritual.* Ithaca, NY: Cornell University Press.

Turner, Victor. 1957. *Schism and Continuity in an African Society; a Study of Ndembu Village Life.* Published on behalf of the Rhodes-Livingstone Institute, Northern Rhodesia, by Manchester University Press, Manchester, England.

Tylor, Edward Burnett. 1871. *Primitive Culture.* London: John Murray.

Van Gennep, Arnold. 2004 [1908]. *The Rites of Passage.* London: Routledge.

Veblen, Thorstein. 1899. *The Theory of the Leisure Class.* New York: Macmillan.

Waitzs, Theodor. 1859. *Anthropologie der naturvölker.* 3 vols. F. Fleischer, Leipzig.

Wallerstein, Immanuel. 2004. *World-Systems Analysis: An Introduction.* Durham, NC: Duke University Press.

Weber, Max. 2015. *Weber's Rationalism and Modern Society.* Translated and edited by Tony Waters and Dagmar Waters. New York: Palgrave Macmillan.

Weber, Max. 2013 [1919]. "The Profession and Vocation of Politics." In *Max Weber: Political Writing*, edited by Peter Lassman and translated by Ronald Speirs. Cambridge, UK: Cambridge University Press.

Weber, Max. 1976 [1897, 1889, 1909]. *Agrarian Sociology of Ancient Civilization.* London: NLB. Atlantic Highlands, NJ: Humanities Press.

Weber, Max. 1968 [1922]. *Economy and Society.* Translated by E. Fischoff et al. New York: Bedminster Press.

Weber, Max. 1963 [1922]. *The Sociology of Religion.* Boston: Beacon Press.

Weber, Max. 1930 [1904–1905, 1920]. *The Protestant Ethic and the Spirit of Capitalism.* London: G. Allen & Unwin, Ltd.

White, Leslie. 2007 [1959]. *The Evolution of Culture.* Walnut Creek, CA: Left Coast Press.

White, Leslie. 1969 [1949]. *The Science of Culture: a Study of Man and Civilization.* New York: Farrar, Straus and Giroux.

White, Tim D., Berhane Asfaw, Yonas Beyene, Yohannes Haile-Selassie, C. Owen Lovejoy, Gen Suwa, and Giday WoldeGabriel. 2009. "*Ardipithecus ramidus* and the Paleobiology of Early Hominids." *Science* 64: 75–86.

Willey, G. R. and J. A. Sabloff. 1980. *A History of American Archaeology.* Second edition. London: Thames and Hudson.

Wolf, Eric. 1982. *Europe and the People Without History.* Berkeley: University of California Press.

"World Languages," Ethnologue: Languages of the World, accessed June 10, 2015, www.ethnologue.com

Wu X, Zhang C, Goldberg P, Cohen D, Pan Y, Arpin T, and Bar-Yosef O. 2012. "Early pottery at 20,000 years ago in Xianrendong Cave, China." *Science.* 336:1696–1700.